MELISSA LOFTUS
LORI SAPPINGTC

THE LITERACY 50

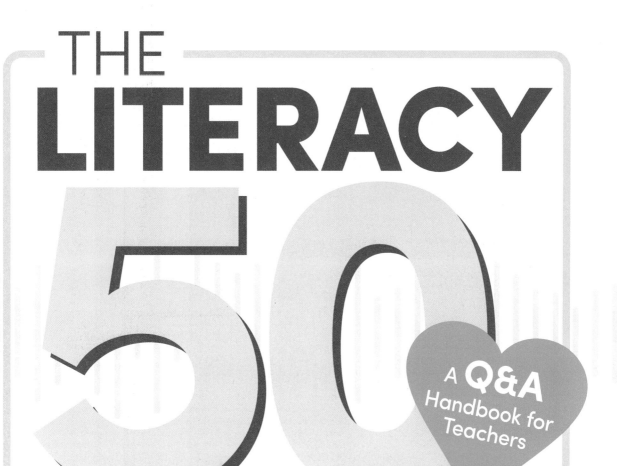

A **Q&A**
Handbook for
Teachers

*Real-World Answers to Questions About
Reading That Keep You Up at Night*

■ **SCHOLASTIC**

For our teacher friends—those we have met in life and through our podcast, and those we have yet to meet. We can't wait to keep learning with you!

President and Publisher: Tara Welty
Editorial Director: Sarah Longhi
Development Editor: Raymond Coutu
Production Editor: Danny Miller
Assistant Editor: Samantha Unger
Creative Director: Tannaz Fassihi
Interior Designer: Maria Lilja

Links to Melissa & Lori Love Literacy podcast powered by Great Minds PBC.

Scholastic is not responsible for the content of third-party websites and does not endorse any site or imply that the information on the site is error-free, correct, accurate, or reliable.

Photos ©: 72 (right): iStock/Getty Images. All other photos © Shutterstock. Icons by The Noun Project.

Credits: 15: "English Vowel Phonemes by Order of Articulation" from *Speech to Print: Language Essentials for Teachers*, Third Edition by Louisa Cook Moats, Ed.D. © 2020 by Paul H. Brookes Publishing Co., Inc., Baltimore. Reprinted by permission; 21: card from *P Is for Paint: A Mnemonic Alphabet Adventure* © Heidi Jane. Used by permission; 44: UFLI Foundations "Scope & Sequence" by Holly B. Lane © University of Florida Literacy Institute. Reprinted by permission; and *Scholastic Ready4Reading®* "Scope & Sequence" © 2023 by Scholastic Inc.; 47: "Your Brain on Reading" © Elise Lovejoy. Used by permission; 50: "Decodable High-Frequency Words" from *Phonics From A–Z* © 2023 by Wiley Blevins. Reprinted by permission of Scholastic Inc.; 55: "Analyzing Spelling Errors" © Shelley Blackwell, Literacy Through Language. Used by permission; 57: *Chimps Can Be Chums* © 2023 by Lefty's Editorial Services. Reprinted by permission of Scholastic Inc.; 60: "Cub Fun" from *Short Reads Decodables* © 2023 by Scholastic Inc.; 80: "Earthquake!" from *Fluency Practice Read-Aloud Plays: Grades 3–4* text © 2006 by Kathleen M. Hollenbeck, illustrations © Scholastic Inc. Reprinted by permission of Scholastic Inc.; 89, 98: "Oral Reading Fluency Norms" by Jan Hasbrouck and Gerald Tindal from "An Update to Compiled ORF Norms" (Technical Report #1702) © 2017 by Behavioral Research and Teaching, University of Oregon. Reprinted courtesy of Dr. Gerald Tindal; 92: "Multidimensional Fluency Rubric" © 1991 by Tim Rasinski and Jerry Zutell. Reprinted by permission. All rights reserved.

1 2 3 4 5 6 7 8 9 10   40   33 32 31 30 29 28 27 26 25 24

Scholastic Inc., 557 Broadway, New York, NY 10012

CONTENTS

Acknowledgments

First and foremost, we want to thank all of our teacher friends who listen to our podcast, *Melissa and Lori Love Literacy*. YOU are the reason this book is possible: your thoughtful questions, your dedication to students, and your hunger for learning. We love learning with you with each and every episode! And, thank you to the 200+ guests we've interviewed for generously sharing your time and expertise with our listeners.

A special thank you to Great Minds for its support. *Wit & Wisdom ELA* and the accompanying professional learning truly help us conceptualize how reading science research translates into classroom practice. Our podcast wouldn't be possible without Andy Azula, Quita Coleman, Lorraine Griffith, Emilie Hughes, Mica Jochim, Brett Juchniewicz, Amanda Norelli, and Rachel Stack.

Thank you to Kareem Weaver, who wrote our foreword and whose endless advocacy for all students is an inspiration to us. He encourages educators everywhere to use evidence-based instructional approaches so all students have the right to read.

We also want to thank the many educators who reviewed our book along the way and provided us with guidance and feedback: Meagan Beam, Mitchell Brookins, Allison Greco, Nancy Hennessy, Kory Jensen, Suzanne Kachura, Julia Lindsey, Kim Lockhart, and Chase Young.

A special thank you to the teachers who shared their hard work with us and allowed us to showcase their talents through pictures and videos: Jaclyn Feuss, Kory Jensen, Elise Lovejoy, Heidi Jane Martin, Heather Monat, Sean Morrisey, and Kristin Poppens.

We also want to thank Ray Coutu, who has the kindest heart in all the land. Thank you for boosting our confidence with countless "you can do it" emails. Also, thank you to Sarah Longhi, Tara Welty, and the entire Scholastic team who made this book possible. It's an honor to contribute to Scholastic's Science of Reading in Practice series.

Last but not least, a special thank you to our families, who supported us as we worked on this book late into the night and super early in the morning. We could not have done it without you!

Foreword by Kareem Weaver

"So what do I do?"

This book is about that question, which every teacher asks—often many times a day. The education landscape can be so complex and confoundingly ambiguous. The theories and research about how children learn to read regularly take center stage in a seemingly endless arc of discovery and engagement. As a result, teachers are often left with more questions than answers about what to do.

This book is a critical offering to the field. It focuses on the nuts and bolts of instruction and answers common questions educators have about what to do and, just as importantly, what to avoid.

That alone makes *The Literacy 50* a must-read.

Since the debut of their popular podcast, Melissa and Lori have promised to focus on the science of reading for students of all ages, and they have delivered on that promise by interviewing researchers and practitioners alike. But their book is different. They've taken the five pillars identified by the National Reading Panel, opened them up, and made them accessible to teachers. They ignore the noise, and focus on winning for kids and the educators who serve them.

Responses to questions such as, "Should I move away from using leveled texts, and, if so, what should I do instead?" must not be relegated to heady conversations and white papers because, among classroom educators and school administrators, those questions are absolute conundrums that touch on the things we've learned in graduate school, the professional assumptions we've held, and the resources we've purchased (often out of our own pockets). Is clear guidance too much to ask?

This book addresses those issues with practitioners' needs in mind. It is filled with answers to real-world conundrums. While the questions the authors pose may keep educators up at night, the answers may help to stem the bottomless pit of school leaders purchasing materials that are not aligned to the evidence about what works best to teach children to read.

We are all painfully aware of the resources educators spend to ensure they and their students have what's needed for learning. The least we can do, as a professional development community, is ensure they are not wasting their precious talent, time, and treasures because the defining questions of their practice remain unanswered. This book answers many of those questions.

So with that, I want to situate *The Literacy 50* in the broader context of social justice. The National Association for the Advancement of Colored People (NAACP) has long identified literacy as a civil right. NAACP's 2014 literacy-related national resolution begins, "WHEREAS, low literacy and functional illiteracy is reaching crisis levels within our society as a whole. Literacy impacts both educational attainment as well as economic status, and low literacy levels can be responsible for unemployment, poverty, academic failure, increased criminal behavior, and poor health outcomes..." Relatedly, The Ontario Human Rights Commission identified literacy, in 2019, as a human rights issue and, as a result of its deep analysis and investigation, made 157 recommendations to promote students' right to read.

Yet, while those are important declarations, social justice lies within the daily reality of teaching and learning. It is birthed from planning, practice, and attention to detail. It is in that spirit that this book was written—a book by educators for educators. By answering real questions from educators about the topics they need to ensure students' civil right to read, this book is a testament to the indomitable spirit of the American educator. Educators have always endeavored to guarantee literacy for all students. The human right to read is sacred, and the quest to secure it is worthy of recognition and gratitude.

Thank you, Melissa and Lori.

—**KAREEM WEAVER**
Co-Founder and Executive Director, Fulcrum
NAACP Oakland's 2nd Vice President and
Education Committee Chair

> *Hi, teacher friend!*
> *We're so glad you're here*
> *to learn with us!*

About Us

In 2018, after many years as English Language Arts teachers, we were both working as district leaders in Baltimore, Maryland, when the district adopted a new knowledge-building curriculum, *Wit & Wisdom* ELA. We worked closely to study its components, participate in professional learning on its implementation, and support teacher colleagues as they prepared to teach this new curriculum. In the process, we learned so much, not only about the curriculum, but also the best ways to teach reading. We had so many "aha" moments together!

Our early days of podcasting from the basement, Lori on the left and Melissa on the right.

On a whim in 2019, Lori came to Melissa with an idea for a podcast, which would give us a place to keep learning and share that learning with others who may have been going through similar mindset shifts. We wanted teachers to know that they weren't alone.

In April of 2019, we recorded our first episode of the *Melissa and Lori Love Literacy* podcast, in Melissa's basement. Since then, we have interviewed over 200 thought leaders, teachers, and administrators and released as many episodes, and we are nearing two million downloads! We have read so much about the best methods for teaching reading and talked about them on the podcast. The thought leaders we have interviewed—including David Liben, Tim Shanahan, and Natalie Wexler— translate the research in a truly accessible way, while the teachers and administrators share what methods look like in the classroom and throughout the building.

Over the years, as the body of research we call the science of reading became more widespread, we began to understand just how complex teaching reading is, and how many misunderstandings there are about it out there. We clearly had not learned everything we needed to in college, even in our master's programs in the teaching of reading. We also realized how methods and materials we had used in the past weren't aligned to reading research.

And here we are now!

Why We Wrote This Book

We wrote this book for many reasons. Here are our main three.

Reason #1: We Have to Get Reading Instruction Right

In our careers, we've seen the impact of poor reading instruction firsthand. When we taught high school and middle school, we had a lot of students coming to us who were struggling. And our schools did not have a clear plan in place for how to help those students get the instruction they needed. In the audio documentary, "Hard Words: Why Aren't Kids Being Taught to Read?" (2018), Emily Hanford reports, "More than 60 percent of American fourth graders are not proficient readers, according to the National Assessment of Educational Progress, and it's been that way since testing began in the 1990s."

Being a proficient reader is essential for students to navigate all their classes in school, to find success in their careers, and to move through life. Literacy leader and activist Kareem Weaver, says, "If you can't read, you're disenfranchised as a collective, as a group, as a community, and individually within families. You can't make your way without reading. It's difficult" (Episode 112). If students are not proficient readers, life is hard and can be traumatic. Psychologist Dr. Steven Dykstra shared with us, "Going to school day after day, week after week, for years while being unable to read, or read well, is frequent and repetitive trauma" (Episode 100).

Teaching according to what reading-science research says works is essential to ensure students' success and well-being. One of our guests, kindergarten teacher

Kristin Poppens, says, "A solid foundation of beginning literacy skills is one of the best gifts I can provide students for future reading success" (Episode 63). We saw in classrooms—and still see—curricular materials and belief systems misaligned to research: leveled reading, workshop models, weak phonics scope and sequences, strategies-only comprehension focus, and too much unmonitored independent reading. In our early years of teaching, we didn't know any better. Now we are committed to doing better. We read current and longstanding research, ask questions, and make sense of what we are learning by talking with each other, experts, teachers, and leaders. We wrote this book to bring together the research on how to teach students to read in a way that respects your busy life.

Reason #2: Good Questions Deserve Good Answers

We see teachers like you asking important questions about how to teach reading well every day on social media. But not every response is necessarily helpful. If you don't know what you don't know, it's hard to know who or what to believe.

There's no other book out there that answers your questions about reading like this one—questions that, indeed, may be keeping you up at night. Most of each chapter's questions came right from listeners of our podcast who wrote to us and entrusted us to answer them wisely.

Each day, we receive many questions from listeners, so we know what is top of mind for teachers who are at different points in their science-of-reading journeys. It is clear from the number of questions in our inbox that teachers care deeply about doing right by their students, and they need an easy-to-read, reliable resource. That's this book: a translation of research by two educators you can trust.

Reason #3: Research Needs to Be Translated in an Accessible Way

It is hard for most researchers to get their findings into the hands of teachers, and it is even harder for most teachers to find time to delve into education journals in their spare time, us included. Not to mention, accessing journals can be costly, and when teachers do access them, the articles can be daunting to read, especially when the information they contain may not be directly connected to practice. It takes a lot of time, effort, and focus to read and interpret research.

The goal of our podcast is to connect what's happening in research and what's happening in the classroom—in other words, to share expert translation of that research. Every episode is not only grounded in research about how to teach reading, but also contains information that is practical and applicable to the classroom. We always have our teacher hats on and try to ask questions you would have to make the content relevant

We have the same goal for this book. We've collected research-based best practices from thought leaders, teachers, and administrators to answer your questions about teaching reading. Most importantly, the Q&As are easy to read and immediately applicable to your daily reality.

About This Book

The Literacy 50 is an easy-to-read, flip-to-what-you-need resource packed with advice informed by reliable research and voices in literacy. We want reading it to feel like popping over to your best teacher-friend's classroom to ask your most pressing professional questions: Is there any research on sound walls? What is the best way to teach phonics in small groups? What makes a text decodable? Why is fluency important? Why should students read grade-level, complex texts, rather than leveled texts? What is the role of vocabulary and knowledge in comprehension?

How It's Organized

In 1997, the U.S. Congress asked the National Institute of Child Health and Human Development and the U.S. Department of Education to establish the National Reading Panel (NRP). The NRP evaluated existing research and evidence to find the best ways of teaching children to read. They reviewed more than 100,000 reading studies and analyzed 432 studies for the report. In 2000, the panel concluded its work and published a 449-page report that clearly addresses effective reading instruction in three critical areas:

1. Alphabetics (phonemic awareness and phonics instruction)
2. Fluency
3. Comprehension (vocabulary and text comprehension instruction)

The Literacy 50 is organized by what are commonly called the "pillars" of those areas (although there is quite a bit of overlap among them). There are five chapters:

Chapter 1: Phonemic Awareness We answer your questions about teaching students the individual sounds they hear in words. We dive into best practices for phonemic awareness instruction, providing insight into teaching with or without letters, sequencing instruction, and using sound walls and other instructional tools.

Chapter 2: Phonics We address questions on orthographic mapping, sight words, and decodable texts in small-group reading instruction, and other topics related to phonics instruction.

Chapter 3: Fluency We dive into some meaty questions about fluency instruction. Specifically, we address the connection between fluency and comprehension, effective fluency practices such as echo reading and Readers' Theater, and how to assess fluency and interpret results.

Chapter 4: Vocabulary We focus on vocabulary development and research-based methods for instruction. We explore the connection between vocabulary and comprehension, the various tiers of words, and tools for teaching.

Chapter 5: Comprehension We answer questions about skills and strategies, how to teach comprehension, and the role knowledge plays in comprehending text.

Each chapter includes 10 frequently asked questions related to each area of reading instruction. For each question, you will see:

- **Question and Answer** To answer the question, we synthesize and translate reading research and learning from our podcast in a brief, easy-to-follow answer.
- **What You Can Do** For each question, we offer ideas for instruction that you can start applying immediately.
- **Check Out Our Podcast** We share episodes to help you learn even more about each question's topic. So grab your cell phone and open your podcast app. You'll want to listen to every episode!
- **Teaching Tool** For most questions, we include an organizer, image, or chart to help you plan instruction and implement it.

How To Use It

While writing this book, we envisioned you—whether you're a teacher, coach, or school or district leader—using it in so many ways: in professional learning book studies and podcast listening groups, as an instructional planning tool, as a handy desk reference, and more. Because the book is organized according to specific areas of reading and designed to highlight questions, it's easy to zoom in on what you need. We're especially interested to learn how you and your school, district, or state use the book, especially the "What You Can Do" and "Teaching Tool" sections, to help connect research to classroom practice.

This book equips you with the science-based information you need to make decisions about instruction... and the resources you need to put that information into practice. We are honored to be joining you on your learning journey.

Melissa ♥ Lori

CHAPTER 1

PHONEMIC AWARENESS

The smallest unit of sounds within words are called phonemes. **Phonemic awareness** refers to the ability to hear and manipulate phonemes within spoken words.

MELISSA'S STORY

My son is four years old and in pre-kindergarten. Like almost all kids his age, he pronounces some words incorrectly. For instance, he says *karana* instead of *piranha*, and *snore* instead of *s'more*. It is fascinating because he is consistent with, and pretty insistent about, those pronunciations. I love listening for them, just noting them (I actually keep a list) and wondering where they come from. For now, it's just kind of funny and cute.

But in the back of my mind, I'm thinking about when he learns to read and spell, and worrying if those mispronunciations will pose challenges for him. Likely, he will have some "aha" moments when he sees a word such as *piranha* in print and says, "Oh, it's a /p/ sound!" But I have kept my eye on his pronunciation of *yellow* as *lellow* because I know that /y/ sound might be tricky for him to pronounce and hear when he starts reading.

Children's spoken language has a considerable impact on how they translate speech into print as they learn to read and spell. That's what this chapter is all about. Let's get started!

Questions That Keep You Up at Night

1.1 "Phonological awareness, phonemic awareness, and phonics, oh my!" What's the difference between them?

1.2 What are the best practices for teaching phonemic awareness?

1.3 Should I name and show letters when I teach phonemic awareness?

1.4 What should I teach first—letter names or letter sounds?

1.5 What are blending and segmenting, and how do I teach them?

1.6 What are deleting and substituting, and how do I teach them?

1.7 Which phonemic awareness skills should I be teaching, in what order, and at what grade level?

1.8 What is the role of language variation in phonemic awareness instruction?

1.9 What are sound walls? How are they different from word walls?

1.10 What's the best way to use sound walls to teach reading?

"Phonological awareness, phonemic awareness, and phonics, oh my!" What's the difference between them?

ANSWER Phonological awareness, phonemic awareness, and phonics all come from the Greek root *phono-*, which means sound or voice, as in *telephone*. And they all work together when children learn to read.

Phonological Awareness Researcher and author Julia Lindsey defines phonological awareness as the ability to hear, manipulate, and generate any kind of sound in language (Episode 120). It is a broad term that encompasses many types of awareness related to words and their sounds, including:

- word awareness: *pancake*
- syllable awareness: /pan/ /cake/
- onset-rime awareness: /p/ /an/　/c/ /ake/
- phonemic awareness: /p/ /ă/ /n/ /k/ /ā/ /k/ (Lane et al., 2001)

Children show word awareness when they understand that phrases or sentences are made up of individual words. They show syllable awareness when they can hear and manipulate each unit of sound in spoken words that contains a vowel. They show onset-rime awareness when they can hear the initial sound before the vowel, which is the onset, and the sound or sounds that follow, which is the rime.

Phonemic Awareness Phonemic awareness is the understanding that spoken words are made up of individual *phonemes*, the smallest units of sound in spoken language. For example, being able to hear that there are three sounds in the word *bug*: /b/, /ŭ/, and /g/. Students must be able to hear, isolate, generate, and manipulate the sounds in words to be able to decode. Professor Matt Burns says, "You really want to get down to the phonemes as quickly as you can because that's what really drives understanding of reading" (Episode 181).

Phonics During phonics instruction, we provide visual representations of phonemes, which are letters or letter combinations known as *graphemes*. There are 44 sounds in English, but there are over 200 ways to represent those sounds. In the word *pancake*, for example, the sound /k/ is represented in two ways: with the letter *c* and the letter *k*. And there are nine other ways to spell words with the sound /k/, even with more than one letter, such as *ck* in *pack* or *ch* in *chorus*! Students must connect the sounds and the letters that represent those sounds to learn to read (Episode 148).

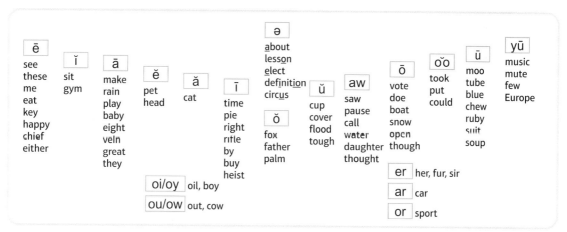

English Vowel Phonemes by Order of Articulation (Moats, 2019)

WHAT YOU CAN DO Here are some fun ways to help children develop phonemic awareness in preschool and early kindergarten:

- Sing songs and read nursery rhymes such as "Twinkle, Twinkle, Little Star" and "Hey Diddle Diddle."
- Play simple rhyming games: "What words rhyme with *boat*? It can even be a silly word!"
- Challenge kids to say tongue twisters that include alliteration such as, "Peter Piper picked a peck of pickled peppers."
- Play simple alliteration games: "How many words can we think of that start with the sound /b/?"
- Play I Spy with sounds: "I spy with my little eye something that starts with the sound /m/."

CHECK OUT OUR PODCAST, EPISODE 120

"Research-Based Routines for Developing Decoding Skills" **with Julia Lindsey** In this episode, Julia Lindsey, author of *Reading Above the Fray*, shares what research says that young readers need to know to help them decode words efficiently.

RELATED EPISODES

- **Episode 148:** "Should You Teach Phonemic Awareness 'In the Dark' or With Print?" with Marjorie Bottari
- **Episode 181:** "What Research Says About Phonemic Awareness" with Matt Burns

What are the best practices for teaching phonemic awareness?

ANSWER Phonemic awareness is one of the best predictors of how well children will learn to read. We had the honor of talking to renowned researcher Louisa Moats, who recommends giving "students the information about what the consonants in the language are and what the vowels in the language are" (Episode 113). From there, she suggests telling students that they are going to learn each of the sounds and letters.

When planning phonemic awareness instruction, keep these things in mind:

- Students benefit from focusing on only one or two phonemic awareness skills at a time. More than that can be overwhelming and is much less effective (Episode 181; Rice et al., 2022).
- Most researchers agree that the amount of time for phonemic awareness instruction should be brief (Erbeli et al., 2024). Louisa Moats and Carol Tolman, authors of *Language Essentials for Teachers of Reading and Spelling (LETRS)*, recommend doing oral-only phonemic awareness activities for about 5 to 10 minutes per day for only 12 to 20 weeks with PreK and kindergarten students (2019).
- Phonemic awareness instruction should be explicit and include clear explanations and teacher modeling (Episode 113; Honig, Diamond, & Gutlohn, 2018). It should provide opportunities for students to practice basic phonemic awareness skills, such as isolating and identifying sounds in words—for example, isolating and identifying the first sound in the word *pot* is /p/. Blending sounds (e.g., putting /p/ /ŏ/ /t/ together to make *pot*) and segmenting words (e.g., separating /p/ /ŏ/ /t/ to isolate each sound in the word *pot*) may deserve more instructional time because they have been widely viewed as the most important for learning to read and spell (Rice et al., 2022). (Read more about blending and segmenting in Question 1.5.)

> "My approach to phoneme awareness is to give the students the information about what the consonants in the language are and what the vowels in the language are… and we're going to learn them one by one."
>
> **—LOUISA MOATS, EPISODE 113**

WHAT YOU CAN DO Julia Lindsey says that using Elkonin boxes, or sound boxes, is an effective strategy to support phonemic awareness instruction. She explains that listening for sounds can be difficult for students. Elkonin boxes help make sounds more concrete and identifiable because students use tokens, such as chips, game pieces, coins, toy cars, or even letters (yes, letters!) to represent individual sounds (Episode 120; Ehri & Roberts, 2006).

Elkonin boxes are easy to create. You can make them yourself, with three or four blank boxes, and laminate them or draw them on a personal whiteboard. Be sure the boxes are large enough for students to move tokens into them. Here are steps for using Elkonin boxes:

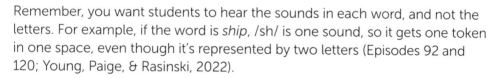

1. Tell students they will push one token into a box for each sound they hear in a word.
2. Pronounce the word slowly to emphasize each phoneme.
3. Have students repeat the word.
4. Ask: "What is the first sound you hear?"
5. Have students move a token into the first box to represent the sound.
6. Continue with the remaining sounds.

Remember, you want students to hear the sounds in each word, and not the letters. For example, if the word is *ship*, /sh/ is one sound, so it gets one token in one space, even though it's represented by two letters (Episodes 92 and 120; Young, Paige, & Rasinski, 2022).

CHECK OUT OUR PODCAST, EPISODE 113

"Reading Is Rocket Science" with Louisa Moats In this episode, Louisa Moats discusses and defines the term "science of reading," while connecting decades of research and theory to classroom practice.

RELATED EPISODES

- **Episode 92:** "Talking About the Literacy Block with Two Early Elementary Teachers" with April Evans and Danielle Hunter
- **Episode 120:** "Research-Based Routines for Developing Decoding Skills" with Julia Lindsey
- **Episode 181:** "What Research Says About Phonemic Awareness" with Matt Burns

Should I name and show letters when I teach phonemic awareness?

ANSWER When you introduce letter-sound correspondences, you are teaching phonics. So it may seem wise to keep instruction in phonemic awareness separate so students can master it first. Surprise! That is not the case. It's actually important to connect letters to sounds quickly. The National Reading Panel (2000) found that instruction in phoneme manipulation using letters helped all readers acquire phonemic awareness faster than instruction without using letters. Instruction using letters also results in better reading outcomes down the line (Episode 181; Clemens et al., 2021). Louisa Moats and Carol Tolman (2019) encourage us to "use letters to represent sounds as soon as young students are ready. Letters reinforce and support phonemic awareness once students have learned to attend to sounds." Children may need some phonemic awareness practice in isolation, but the most important work happens with letters.

Instructional simultaneity means addressing more than one teaching target at a time. This practice is particularly beneficial when teaching reading foundational skills such as phonemic awareness, phonics, and fluency (Duke, Lindsey, & Wise, 2023). As children start to identify initial phonemes, such as /b/ in *bug* and *bat*, teach them the letter that is most commonly associated with that sound—in this case, /b/, is represented by the letter *b* (Piasta & Hudson, 2022). So it's not so much about whether or not to use letters when teaching phonemic awareness, but rather *when* to introduce them. As soon as kids can handle letters and sounds at the same time, we should help them to connect the two (Episode 120).

Ernesto Ortiz, Jr., school leader from Warminster, Pennsylvania, told us how he and his teachers maximize their time for phonemic awareness instruction, even if it's only 5 to 10 minutes a day. They connect the sound to letters as quickly as possible (Episode 141).

> "What we're trying to get is the recognition of the letters and the immediate, automatic millisecond attachment of sound that we need in order to become fluent."
>
> —TAMI REIS-FRANKFORT, EPISODE 147

WHAT YOU CAN DO Researcher Susan Brady suggests introducing letters as soon as students have a solid awareness of just a few phonemes (2020). As you continue introducing students to phonemes, continue introducing them to letters as well, starting with the letters that most commonly represent the sounds. Then introduce other graphemes that represent those sounds. For instance, you might start by introducing the letter *k* once students have awareness of the sound /k/, such as in *kit*. Later, you can introduce the letter *c* and note when it represents /k/, such as in *cat*, or the letter combination *ck*, as in *back*.

Elementary teachers Danielle Hunter and April Evans have students use Elkonin boxes to hit the phoneme processor, and then connect the sound to letters by writing the word. They talk to the students about the meaning of words and how it connects to what they're reading (Episode 92).

In a lesson, you might:

1. Show students the letter *b* and say the sound /b/.
2. Orally blend sounds in a word that includes /b/, such as /b/ /a/ /t/ = bat.
3. Write the word *bat*.
4. Read a decodable text or word list that features the sound /b/.

Students practice writing letters that connect with sounds and blending sounds with letters.

CHECK OUT OUR PODCAST, EPISODE 92

"Talking About the Literacy Block with Two Early Elementary Teachers" with April Evans and Danielle Hunter In this episode, two veteran teachers from Aurora, Colorado, discuss their literacy blocks and how they use Elkonin boxes with and without letters.

RELATED EPISODES

- **Episode 120:** "Research-Based Routines for Developing Decoding Skills" with Julia Lindsey
- **Episode 141:** "Literacy Leaders as Agents of Change" with Ernesto Ortiz, Jr.
- **Episode 181:** "What Research Says About Phonemic Awareness" with Matt Burns

What should I teach first, letter names or letter sounds?

ANSWER Many American children are taught their letter names at a young age. Louisa Moats (1998) says, "One of the most fundamental flaws found in almost all phonics programs, including traditional ones, is that they teach the code backwards. That is, they go from letter to sound instead of from sound to letter." She states that a focus on letter names without a clear understanding of the sounds they represent can confuse students when they are learning to read and spell.

Therefore, decoding instruction should focus on the letter-sound correspondences, so students are actively using their knowledge of phonemes.

Knowing letter names gives students and teachers a common language to talk about the sounds that a grapheme can represent.

> "Learning the alphabet can be fun, right? We want to make this sort of abstract process meaningful and fun."
>
> **–CAROLYN STROM, EPISODE 164**

Auditory drill in Ms. Lockhart's classroom, a French immersion teacher in Ontario, Canada.

Children benefit when they are taught letter names and sounds simultaneously (Episode 180; Ehri, 1995). Letter knowledge and phonemic awareness are the best predictors of how well children learn to read during their first two years of school (Piasta, 2023; Piasta & Hudson, 2022; Jones, Clark, & Reutzel, 2012).

WHAT YOU CAN DO A common practice in kindergarten is teaching a "letter of the week." But you can introduce letters at a much faster pace, closer to three new letters (names and sounds!) per week, with continued practice of letter names and sounds you've introduced previously (Piasta & Hudson, 2022).

Although there is no research on the best order of teaching letters and their sounds, professor Shayne Piasta shares some possible sequences:

1. **Letters that appear in children's first name:** Children usually learn the letters in their first names easily and quickly, especially the first letter.

2. **Letter frequency:** Children usually learn letters that appear frequently in print, such as *e*, *t*, and *a*, more quickly than those that appear less frequently, such as *z*, *q*, and *j*.

3. **Letter name pronunciation:** Children usually learn a letter name and sound more easily if they can hear the letter's sound in its name. So you may start with *b* because you can hear the sound /b/ in the letter name, but leave *w* for later because it doesn't contain the sound /w/.

(Episode 180; Reutzel, 2015)

No matter the order in which you introduce letter names and sounds, you can use a fun research-based strategy called embedded mnemonics. An embedded mnemonic is when the letter is embedded into a picture that reflects its sound. For example, the letter *o* would be within a picture of an octopus, so children simultaneously see the shape of the letter *o* and a visual representation of a word that starts with it. According to literacy researcher Tim Shanahan (2021), using embedded mnemonics reduces the number of repetitions students need "to learn the letter names and sounds, with less confusion, better long-term memory, and greater ability to transfer or apply this knowledge in reading and spelling" (Episode 164; Piasta & Hudson, 2022).

O is for octopus.

From *P Is for Paint: A Mnemonic Alphabet Adventure* by Heidi Jane

CHECK OUT OUR PODCAST, EPISODE 180

"Teaching the Alphabet" with Shayne Piasta In this episode, Shayne Piasta, professor and researcher at The Ohio State University, discusses best practices for teaching alphabet knowledge. She tells us what research suggests about teaching letter names and sounds, and why teaching a letter a week may not be effective. She also offers concrete strategies for classroom practice.

RELATED EPISODES

- **Episode 147:** "What Is Speech to Print?" with Marnie Ginsberg and Tami Reis Frankfort
- **Episode 164:** "Misconceptions about Learning to Read" with Carolyn Strom

TEACHING TOOL

Alphabet Lesson Template

Alphabet lessons enable you to teach letter names, sounds, and forms explicitly. In these lessons, you introduce students to and have them identify the letter name and sound so they recognize the letter in speech and text, and can produce the letter form in writing.

Be sure to teach both the uppercase and lowercase forms of letters. As always, keep an eye on your students' needs so you can move more quickly or slow down and increase or decrease the number of times students see each letter (Jones, Clark, & Reutzel, 2012).

ALPHABET LESSON TEMPLATE

Review	**1 minute**	**Review previously taught letters and sounds.**
STEP 1 **Letter Name**	1–2 minutes	"Today, you will be learning the name and sound of the letter *b*, and how to write it." Show or write the uppercase letter *B*. "This is the uppercase letter *B*." Show or write the lowercase letter *b*. "This is the lowercase letter *b*." Practice naming the letter. Point to the uppercase and lowercase letters and ask students to say the letter name.
STEP 2 **Letter Sound**	1–2 minutes	The letter *b* represents the sound /b/. Explain how to produce the sound /b/. Use a sound wall to support this explanation: • lips are pressed together, teeth are apart inside your mouth, pucker your lips, when your mouth opens a small puff of air is released, vocal cords are vibrating The letter *b* represents the /b/ sound. "Say the /b/ sound." Allow students time to practice forming the sound.
STEP 3 **Letter Recognition**	2–3 minutes	"Now, let's see if we can hear the letter *b*." Show a picture of a bed or embedded mnemonic. "What sound do you hear in the beginning of *bed*?" If students can't produce the sound say, "*b b bed*." Tell students, "you try, *b b bed*." Then show students a new picture card or embedded mnemonic with the same beginning sound:. Ask: "What sound do you hear in the beginning of the word *ball*?" "Now, let's see if we can find the letter *b*." Provide students with a text that has just a few words on each page. Have students find the letter in print, and say the letter and the sound.
STEP 4 **Letter Writing**	4–5 minutes	"Let me show you how to write the letter." Model and provide description and hints about how to write the uppercase *B* and lowercase *b*. "Let's practice writing the uppercase letter *B* and lowercase letter *b*." Give students the opportunity to practice the letter formation by tracing the letter, writing the letter on the carpet, in the air, on their hand, or on a whiteboard. Have students say the sound multiple times as they form the letter.
Review	1 minute	Show the letter. Ask: "What is the letter? What sound does the letter *b* represent?" Show a picture or embedded mnemonic. Say: "*B* is for *bug*." Have students repeat.

(Adapted from Jones, Clark, & Reutzel, 2012, Lindsey, 2022, and Kristin Poppens)

Download the "Alphabet Lesson Template."

What are blending and segmenting, and how do I teach them?

ANSWER More than any other phonological awareness skills, blending sounds into words and segmenting words into individual sounds are crucial to learning to read and spell (Episode 181; Honig, Diamond, & Gutlohn, 2018).

Blending

Blending is an essential skill for students who are learning to decode words (Kilpatrick, 2016; Honig, Diamond, & Gutlohn, 2018; Brady, 2020). When blending phonemes, you hear the individual sounds separately and combine them to form a recognizable word. For example, you might slowly say the sounds /p/ /ĭ/ /t/, and students would recognize that the word is *pit* by blending the sounds together. Blending tends to be easier than segmenting for most students.

Segmenting

Segmenting is separating a word into individual sounds, or phonemes, and saying each one. For example, you might say *pit*, and students would identify each sound: /p/ /ĭ/ /t/. Students can respond in various ways: by articulating sounds, tapping out sounds, counting sounds, using Elkonin boxes, and so forth. Segmenting is an essential skill for students who are learning how to spell, or encode, words (Episode 148; Honig, Diamond, & Gutlohn, 2018).

You can do some quick practice blending and segmenting syllables or onsets and rimes if students need that level of practice before doing the work with phonemes. To blend syllables, you might slowly say *pan* and then *cake* and ask students what word they hear: *pancake*. Similarly, to blend onsets and rimes, you might say /b/ and then *each* and ask what word

Segmenting words into phonemes in Kim Lockhart's classroom.

they hear: *beach*. When segmenting syllables, say a word and ask students to say the syllables they hear, and when segmenting onsets and rimes, say a word and ask students to say the onset and then the rime. Keep in mind, they don't need to master blending and segmenting skills at the syllable and onset-rime level before applying them at the phoneme level. You want students to spend the bulk of their phonemic awareness time blending and segmenting at the phoneme level.

WHAT YOU CAN DO As always, make it explicit! Explain blending and segmenting to students, show them how to do it, allow them plenty of practice, and provide immediate feedback.

Here are some ideas for teaching students to blend and segment phonemes:

- **Sing the Sounds** Kristin Poppens, a kindergarten teacher from Cedar Falls, Iowa, loves to sing in her classroom (Episode 63). For blending, she suggests that you pick a word, sing one sound at a time, and ask students to guess the word. You can increase the fun by giving students a clue to the word before singing: "I'm thinking of an animal" and then sing the sounds /p/ /ĭ/ /g/ for *pig*. For segmenting, give students the word and let them sing the sounds.

CHECK OUT OUR PODCAST, EPISODE 63

"Kindergarten Teacher Reaches 100% Success Using Evidence-Based Practices" with Kristin Poppens

In this episode, Kristin Poppens tells us her story about learning and changing her instruction after 10 years in the classroom. After using evidence-based practices for less than six months, her students reached end-of-year benchmarks with 100 percent success.

RELATED EPISODES

- **Episode 148:** "Should You Teach Phonemic Awareness 'In the Dark' or With Print?" with Marjorie Bottari
- **Episode 181:** "What Research Says About Phonemic Awareness" with Matt Burns

- **Speak "Robot"** Louisa Moats and Carol Tolman (2019) recommend robot talk where you pick a word, say one sound at a time in a robot voice, and have students guess the word. Or give students the word and have them say its sounds in a robot voice (Yopp, 1992; Chard & Dickson, 1999).

- **Use Manipulatives** Use connectable blocks to represent sounds. Students connect the blocks as they blend sounds and take them apart as they segment sounds. Students can also use a toy car as they blend sounds— just have them drive the car across each sound as they blend them to form a word. Or they can use pop-it bubble poppers to segment words by pressing one bubble for every sound they hear.

TEACHING TOOL

Rime Mats

The kindergarten team from Hansen Elementary in Cedar Falls, Iowa, created a tool called Rime Mats. They use them with their students to practice blending with letters as a bridge between phonemic awareness and decoding. The onset is the initial sound of a word (example: /p/ in *pan* or /sh/ in *ship*) and the rime refers to the sounds that follow the onset, usually a vowel and final consonants (example: *an* in *pan* or *ip* in *ship*). You populate the Rime Mat with rimes that students know based on what they have been taught. Then give students a letter on a card or sticky note to put in front, such as *s* or *d*. Students place the letter in front of the rime, blend the sounds of the letters, and decide whether it is a real word. For example, students can use the letter *d* six times on the Rime Mat shown here to make *dunk*, *dash*, *ding*, *dill*, *dock*, and *dump*.

What are deleting and substituting, and how do I teach them?

ANSWER Deleting and substituting, along with other phonemic awareness skills such as reversing, are all types of manipulation, which means students make changes to words based on their knowledge of spoken language.

Deleting

Phoneme deletion refers to being able to recognize what letter combination remains when one phoneme is removed from a word. For example, you might tell a student, "Say *cup*. Now say *cup* without saying /k/." This prompts the student to recognize that the word *up* remains. Deletion can be that basic or more complex. For example, you might ask a student to delete the /p/ from *spoke* to determine whether he or she recognizes that the word *soak* remains. If this activity is done orally, the different spellings of *spoke* and *soak* still work (Honig, Diamond, & Gutlohn, 2018; Brady, 2020).

Substituting

Phoneme substitution refers to being able to replace one phoneme with another. For example, you might ask a student to change the word *lip* by substituting /p/ with /t/ to determine whether the student hears the new word: *lit* (Honig, Diamond, & Gutlohn, 2018; Kilpatrick, 2016). Remember the song "Apples and Bananas," where you change all the vowel sounds in a word or phrase to one vowel sound (for example, "ee-ples and bee-nee-nees" and "oh-ples and bo-no-nos")? It's a perfect example of substituting phonemes! Try to stick with real words when you're working on substituting with your students, though.

Deleting and substituting have come to be known as "advanced phonemic awareness," a term popularized by David Kilpatrick in his book *Equipped for Reading Success* (2016), and there has been some debate around it. Some people think students must master these advanced phonemic awareness skills. However, Kilpatrick states that once students can blend and segment phonemes, they should practice these skills in the context of reading and writing, and we should use advanced phonemic awareness for students with phonological deficits. More research needs to be done to support the benefits of these skills, even for older, struggling readers (Shanahan, 2021).

WHAT YOU CAN DO Marnie Ginsberg, founder of Reading Simplified, introduced us to the term "set for variability." Imagine a student is decoding the word *blow*. When she pronounces the word, she says the word as /blau/, rhyming with the word *plow*. This is an understandable misreading of the word since those graphemes could represent those phonemes. But after she says the word as /blau/, she immediately knows she has mispronounced the word and corrects the pronunciation. The key is that she has flexibility to manipulate the sounds in that word to read it as a word she knows: /bloh/. This is where substituting phonemes comes into play when reading (Episode 147; Vadasy et al., 2022).

> "If I can blend automatically, if I can segment automatically, if I can manipulate, where does my cognitive load go? To the many different ways I can represent those sounds with print."
>
> —MARJORIE BOTTARI, EPISODE 148

How can you help students increase their cognitive flexibility?

- Continue to build students' oral-language vocabulary, especially for students whose first language is not English. (See Question 4.4 for more information.)
- Teach students the most common spelling patterns and explicitly show them differences that may be confusing. Specifically, show them that:
  - words that are spelled the same can be pronounced differently, such as *blow*, *tow*, *crow*, *brow*, *plow*, and *cow*.
  - words that contain similar sounds can be spelled differently (homophones), such as *blow*, *so*, and *toe*.
- Guide students to correct mispronunciations while reading. Here's an example:
  - Ask: "Is that a word? Does that make sense?"
  - Point out the mispronounced letter sound and ask: "What other sound could this letter (or these letters) represent?"
  - If students don't know, tell them the sound and have them read again.
  - Ask again: "Is that a word? Does that make sense?"

(Ginsberg, 2019)

TEACHING TOOL

Letter-Sound Anchor Charts

As you are teaching letter patterns, tell students that the same letter or letter combinations can represent different sounds. Some of these will be pretty easy for students to learn. For example, c typically represents the /s/ sound or /k/ sound. But others, especially vowels and vowel teams, won't be so easy. So you may want to create anchor charts to help students learn the different ways a grapheme can be pronounced.

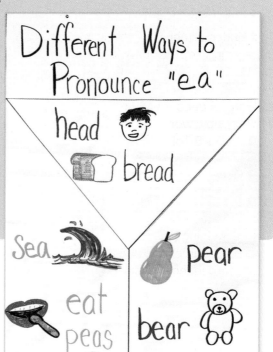

Which phonemic awareness skills should I be teaching, in what order, and at what grade level?

ANSWER Kindergarten teacher Kristin Poppens shared one of her favorite sayings with us: "Go as slow as you need to, but as fast as you can" (Episode 115). There is a general developmental sequence of phonemic awareness skills, and it's important to know where children are, so you know whether to intervene quickly or keep moving forward.

In preschool and early kindergarten, children typically develop phonological awareness skills related to syllable segmentation, rhyming, and initial sound isolation. You might rhyme words and count syllables with students, but don't take too much time doing that because they are not prerequisite skills for reading. In kindergarten, start with initial sound isolation, or identifying the first sounds in a word (e.g., /b/ for *big*, /ch/ for *chat*) (Episode 115; Moats & Tolman, 2019).

Most kindergartners will not be reading and spelling when they arrive at the start of the year. They may have some phonological awareness (rhyming, syllables, etc.) but less phonemic awareness (individual sounds). That's why, at this age, phonemic awareness instruction typically benefits all children. To prepare students for decoding and spelling, focus on blending sounds and segmenting single-syllable words without consonant blends (e.g., *sap*, but not *snap*) (Brady, 2020; Moats & Tolman, 2019).

In first grade, some students may be reading and spelling, so they may not need much instruction in phonemic awareness. For students who are not reading and spelling, give them more time to practice blending sounds and segmenting basic words orally. Beginning in first grade and into second grade, spend more time segmenting and blending using letters. (Read more about segmenting and blending in Question 1.5.)

> "Go as slow as you need to, but as fast as you can."
>
> —KRISTIN POPPENS, EPISODE 115

WHAT YOU CAN DO Here are some grade-specific, evidence-based ideas for building phonemic awareness.

PreK and Beginning Kindergarten

- Read books that contain rhyming, such as *One Day in the Eucalyptus, Eucalyptus Tree*, and alliteration, such as *Pete the Cat and the Perfect Pizza Party* and *In the Small, Small Pond*.
- Make silly alliterative sentences: "Jazmin jumped for joy and drank juice with Jacob."
- Find words that have the same first letter as students' names: "What's the first sound in Mariana? What else starts with /m/?"
- Say a word and have students think of words that rhyme with it.
- Tap and count the syllables in the word.

Kindergarten and First Grade

- Use Elkonin boxes to segment sounds. (See Question 1.2 for details.)
- Say the sounds of words slowly and have students blend them together to say the word. Make it fun by calling it "snail talk" or "robot talk," or by singing the words and their parts. (See Question 1.5 for details.)

Second and Third Grade

- Have students blend sounds in single-syllable words with four or more sounds.
- Build word chains or word ladders where students change phonemes in words to build new words: *mat > cat > cap > tap > tip*. Tim Rasinski's *Daily Word Ladders* books are great resources.

CHECK OUT OUR PODCAST, EPISODE 181

"What Research Says About Phonemic Awareness" with Matt Burns
In this episode, Matt Burns discusses the most impactful ways to teach phonemic awareness, provides practical takeaways for teachers, and recommends additional resources.

RELATED EPISODE

- **Episode 115:** "Kindergarten Team Reaches (Nearly) 100% Success Using Evidence-Based Practices" with Kristin Poppens

What is the role of language variation in phonemic awareness instruction?

ANSWER Researcher and scholar Julie Washington shares that there are many variations of the English language, such as General American English (GAE), Appalachian English, African American English (AAE), Southern English, and Midwestern English, and every English speaker grows up learning to speak some variation of the language (Episode 151). We like the term "language variation" because it is neutral. It doesn't imply that one variation is superior to another.

How does this connect to phonemic awareness? We learn to read by matching spoken language to written text. So the further students' language variation is from the language they need to learn to read at school, the greater the cognitive load will be. If you recognize the differences in the language students bring to school, you can teach the skills they need to learn to read more effectively (Washington & Seidenberg, 2021).

Imagine a student who speaks AAE segmenting words into individual sounds. That student might typically pronounce the word *gold* without the final sound. So, the student might segment the word into three sounds: /g/ /o/ /l/. When there are differences between what students know from the speech they bring from home and the written words they see at school, navigating both language systems can be challenging (Washington, Lee-James, & Stanford, 2023).

WHAT YOU CAN DO How can you respect children's home languages while helping them gain proficiency with the classroom language, typically GAE, to develop reading and writing skills? Here are some steps you can take.

Know the Students in Front of You—and Refrain From Judgment!

Listen for how students pronounce sounds, especially vowels, and words. Notice if they miss or substitute sounds in GAE. As you listen, remember that it is possible to help students learn GAE without sending negative messages about their spoken language variation. Literacy leader Mitchell Brookins reminds us that if children hear that their language is wrong instead of different, it can cause them to see an aspect of themselves or their community as inferior (Episode 75).

Learn About Language Variations

Once you recognize your students' language variations, learn as much as you can about their common rules and patterns. Think about how the rules and patterns might impact students' learning about phonemic awareness. What sounds might they hear differently? What sounds might they struggle to hear at all?

Address Differences, Not "Errors"

Think about how to respond to language variations constructively. Point out differences between GAE and variations. For example, if you have students whose home language is Spanish, and who are just learning English phonology, you may want to draw their attention to sounds made in English that are not made in Spanish, such as the consonant digraphs *sh*, *th*, *wh*, and *ph*.

> "We need to allow children to use the language that they know to support learning to read."
>
> —JULIE WASHINGTON, EPISODE 151

Elkonin boxes can help students hear the differences in the sounds in GAE and their language variations. AAE speakers may reduce final phoneme sounds, so students may only move three markers into a box for the word *past* /p/ /a/ /s/. This is the perfect opportunity to teach students that there are four sounds in the word *past* /p/ /a/ /s/ /t/ in GAE (Pittman, Rice, Garza, & Guerra, 2023). In this case, Mitchell told us he would have the students use Elkonin boxes to spell both versions of the word to affirm the home and school language (Episode 75).

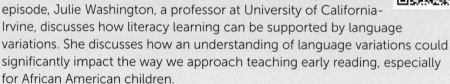

CHECK OUT OUR PODCAST, EPISODE 151

"Science of Reading for ALL Students: Language Variation and Reading" with Julie Washington In this episode, Julie Washington, a professor at University of California–Irvine, discusses how literacy learning can be supported by language variations. She discusses how an understanding of language variations could significantly impact the way we approach teaching early reading, especially for African American children.

RELATED EPISODE

- **Episode 75:** "How Do Language Variants Impact Teaching Reading to African American Students?" with Mitchell Brookins

AAE Phonological Features

AAE is a rule-governed language. When students come to school speaking AAE, they likely know all those rules. The rules are variations of GAE. You can affirm what students already know and build on it to bridge the two language variations as they learn to read.

The following features of AAE are common features that can impact the way speakers of AAE hear words being pronounced. Note that these are common patterns found by researchers, but not all speakers of AAE will exhibit all of these features.

AAE PHONOLOGICAL FEATURES	
Description	**Example**
Deleting the past tense -*ed* marker from words	• "He *jump* over the fence" instead of "He *jumped* over the fence."
Deleting plural and possessive *s*	• "She put on her glass" instead of "She put on her glasses." • "John house" instead of "John's house"
Dropping final *r*	• *foe* instead of *four* • *poe* instead of *pour*
Dropping final *g*	• *runnin* instead of *running* • *playin* instead of *playing*
Consonant cluster reduction	• *col* instead of *cold* • *pas* instead of *past*
Transposing consonant clusters	• *aks* instead of *ask*
Replacing /th/ with /f/, /v/, /t/, or /d/	• *wif* instead of *with* or *wit* instead of *with* • *smoov* instead of *smooth* • *dis* instead of *this*
Merging i/e	• The vowel sound in *pen* and *pin* sound the same. • The vowel sound in *feel* and *fill* sound the same.
Neutralizing diphthongs	• *oil* sounds like *all* • *our* sounds like *are*

Download the "AAE Phonological Features" table.

(Adapted from Washington & Seidenberg, 2021; Gatlin-Nash, 2023; Episode 151)

What are sound walls? How are they different from word walls?

ANSWER Sound walls and word walls are classroom displays designed to support language development—but their similarities pretty much stop there.

Sound Walls

Sound walls focus on the 44 phonemes of the English language. Their purpose is to help students connect sounds to letters, and phonemes to graphemes. You'll often find two walls, one for consonant sounds and one for vowel sounds. They typically include articulation images next to each phoneme that show what the mouth looks like when making the sound the phoneme represents.

Word Walls

Word walls contain high-frequency words and/or content words grouped alphabetically by the 26 letters of the alphabet. Teachers typically add words to the wall as they introduce the words throughout the year. Marjorie Bottari (2020) explains that word walls can cause confusion when you place a word such as *know* under the letter *k* because the initial sound is /n/. Tim Shanahan believes word walls are not helpful for learning to decode or spell, but they are potentially valuable for developing vocabulary (2021). (See Question 4.7 for more information on word walls.)

> "The sound wall is not the main event in my classroom—structured literacy is the main event. The sound wall is a reflection of what's happening in the classroom."
>
> **—LINDSAY KEMENY, EPISODE 80**

WHAT YOU CAN DO Sound walls are very popular. As with word walls, researchers have not yet proven whether they are beneficial (Episode 71), but they seem to help students learn letter-sound correspondences.

Sound walls should be created over time, as students learn the sounds and the corresponding letters and letter combinations. At the beginning of kindergarten, introduce the most common grapheme that represents each sound. For instance, for /n/, introduce the letter *n*. Once you've introduced all the phonemes, gradually add spelling patterns at appropriate locations on the sound wall. Through the primary grades, add less common graphemes that represent the sound, such as *kn*, *gn*, and even *pn* and *mn* for /n/.

Sound walls typically contain visuals, including:

- **Sound Cards:** You will need 43 cards that show the sound of each phoneme, such as /b/ or /sh/ (25 consonant sounds and 18 vowel sounds), along with a word that contains the phoneme and a picture clue.

- **Articulation Cards:** You will need 24 cards for 13 consonant sounds and 11 vowel sounds that feature pictures of the mouth making their sounds. Why not 43 cards? For some voiced and unvoiced letter pairs, such as /t/ and /d/, articulation changes, but mouth placement doesn't, so separate cards aren't needed. You can purchase these cards in sets, use the ones that come with your curriculum, or create your own by taking pictures of your mouth or students' mouths articulating letter sounds.

- **Letter Cards:** Once you've introduced a sound, teach the most common grapheme for that sound. As you connect phonemes to graphemes in phonics instruction, add cards to the sound wall. The cards you need depend on your grade level and your phonics scope and sequence. For instance, you will likely start pretty simple in kindergarten with consonants and short vowels and add more complex spelling patterns in first and second grade (Episode 80; Dahlgren, 2020; Novelli & Sayeski, 2022; Stollar, 2020).

Sound Card

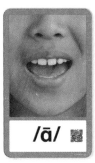

Articulation Card

CHECK OUT OUR PODCAST, EPISODE 80

"A Primary Teacher's Perspective on Science of Reading, Small Group Instruction, and Sound Walls" with Lindsay Kemeny In this episode, Lindsay Kemeny, primary teacher from Utah and author of *7 Mighty Moves*, takes a deep dive into her evidence-based, small-group time. She talks about sound walls and how she and her students use theirs.

RELATED EPISODES

- **Episode 71:** "Science of Reading: Decodable Texts, Sound Walls, & the Aim of Early Literacy, Part 2," with Julia Lindsey
- **Episode 185:** "Understanding the How and Why of Sound Walls" with Mary Dahlgren

TEACHING TOOL

Sound Walls That Sing

Check out these sound walls in a kindergarten classroom! You can start with a blank wall and build the sound wall one phoneme at a time, as you introduce them. You can also create the whole sound wall and cover each of the parts until you introduce them to students. Teachers who are lacking space have also been creative and used tri-fold boards which they take out when needed. Keep the visuals simple and easy to see. Nothing fancy. Think black, sans-serif letters on a solid background.

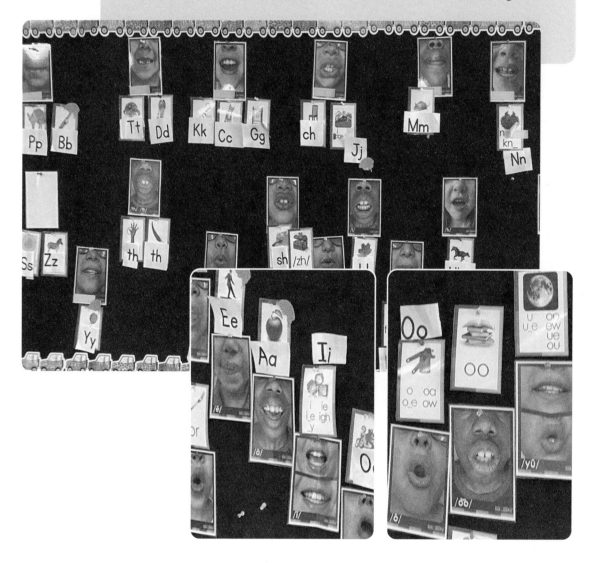

What's the best way to use sound walls to teach reading?

ANSWER Julie Washington says that "reading and language are intertwined," and sound walls can support decoding and spelling instruction by bridging the gap between abstract sounds in language and concrete letters for reading (Episode 151). But you have to use it! Just putting up a sound wall is not helpful to students, no matter how beautiful you make it.

It is important for students to listen for individual phonemes in words. A sound wall can help them produce those sounds and connect speech to print. It is a tool that you and your students can refer to that helps them solidify sound-symbol correspondences.

Although there is not currently research specifically supporting the use of sound walls, there is some research that shows that teaching students articulatory features supports students' phonemic awareness, letter-sound knowledge, and decoding skills. Articulation means how the mouth looks and feels when producing specific sounds. Lindsay Kemeny helps her students by drawing awareness to what's happening with their mouths when they say a sound and connect it to a specific letter or letter combination (Episode 80; Boyer & Ehri, 2011; Lane & Contesse, 2022). (Read more about sound walls in Question 1.9.)

WHAT YOU CAN DO When you introduce a phoneme, model how to make the sound, point to the articulation card on the wall, and teach the most common grapheme or graphemes to spell the sound. Students look at the articulation card for each phoneme and talk about how the lips, tongue, or teeth are in a particular place. From there, add the sound and grapheme on the sound wall (Episode 80; Bottari, 2020; Dahlgren, 2020; Novelli & Sayeski, 2022).

Use Articulation Cards

When you introduce a phoneme, have students focus on what their mouths are doing as they produce it before pointing to the corresponding articulation card on the sound wall. Your school's speech language pathologist (SLP) can be a helpful resource for understanding how to teach articulatory features, which many of us did not learn in our pre-service course work. The Hansen Elementary kindergarten team from Cedar Falls, Iowa, worked closely with their SLP to learn what the tongue, lips, and teeth do when making specific sounds, and whether the sounds are voiced or unvoiced. For instance, they learned that to make the /k/ and /g/ sounds, the mouth position is the same, however, the vocal cords are not making any sound for the /k/ sound, but they are engaged to make the /g/ sound (Iowa Department of Education, 2023).

Use Mirrors

Louisa Moats encourages us to have students look in the mirror when they say a sound to build mouth awareness (Episode 113; Moats & Tolman, 2019). Give each child a handheld mirror. As they watch themselves articulate a sound, have them think about whether their mouths are open or closed, and the placement of tongue, teeth, and/or lips. Do they notice, for instance, that their mouths are closed and lips are pressed together when making the sound /m/? Then give students words to say in the mirror and determine which ones start with that sound (e.g., *monkey*, *milk*, *hat*). Hansen Elementary kindergarten teacher Marisa Bauer also has her students use mirrors to make sure their mouths are in the correct position for each sound before they articulate that sound (Iowa Department of Education, 2023).

> "It's important to actually be aware of all 44 speech sounds rather than just 26 letters."
>
> —MARY DAHLGREN, EPISODE 185

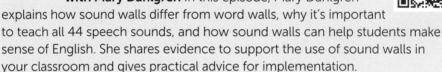

CHECK OUT OUR PODCAST, EPISODE 185

"Understanding the How and Why of Sound Walls" with Mary Dahlgren In this episode, Mary Dahlgren explains how sound walls differ from word walls, why it's important to teach all 44 speech sounds, and how sound walls can help students make sense of English. She shares evidence to support the use of sound walls in your classroom and gives practical advice for implementation.

RELATED EPISODES

- **Episode 80:** "A Primary Teacher's Perspective on Science of Reading, Small Group Instruction, and Sound Walls" with Lindsay Kemeny
- **Episode 113:** "Reading Is Rocket Science" with Louisa Moats
- **Episode 151:** "Science of Reading for ALL Students: Language Variation and Reading" with Julie Washington
- **Episode 186:** "Top Tips for Using Sound Walls" with Christina Winter

TEACHING TOOL

Articulatory Features

Don't spend a lot of time on the sound wall during instruction. Draw students' awareness to it at appropriate points in your instruction and keep moving. Don't wait until you have "perfected" the wall. Just give it a try. Work with colleagues who want to try sound walls and share ideas and experiences. Reach out to your Speech Language Pathologist for help, who will likely love sharing knowledge on this topic (Episodes 80 and 115; Stollar, 2020).

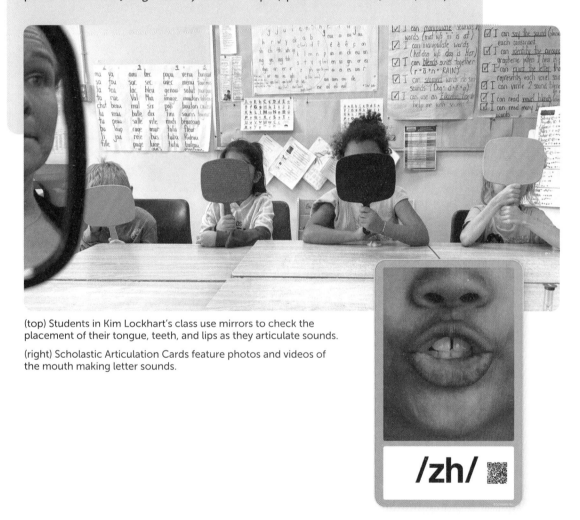

(top) Students in Kim Lockhart's class use mirrors to check the placement of their tongue, teeth, and lips as they articulate sounds.

(right) Scholastic Articulation Cards feature photos and videos of the mouth making letter sounds.

CHAPTER 2

PHONICS

Phonics instruction develops a solid understanding of the relationships between letters and sounds, so students can decode and spell words.

LORI'S STORY

Early in my career, I taught high schoolers who struggled with reading. As time passed, and more and more kids were coming to me, I wondered what was happening at the elementary- and middle-school levels. How were these students being passed along without showing mastery of basic reading skills?

After two years in that role, I made a meteoric leap to second grade. News flash: Things weren't any better there! Students were still struggling to read on grade level. I used the reading program I was handed, but it didn't help me reteach what my students hadn't learned or fill gaps in their learning. At professional development sessions, I heard over and over again statements like, "Give them time, they'll get it," and "Help them find the right book, and it will come together." I poured my heart and soul into organizing my book bins by genre, topic, and text complexity, hoping for the magic to happen. But it never did for way too many of my kids. And I was frustrated, discouraged, and confused about what to do next. Does this resonate? If so, read on!

Questions That Keep You Up at Night

2.1 I keep hearing about the importance of systematic and explicit phonics instruction. What does that mean?

2.2 What is orthographic mapping? I'm not sure I understand what that term means.

2.3 What is the difference between sight words and high-frequency words?

2.4 What are heart words? How do I teach them?

2.5 What is the relationship between spelling and phonics?

2.6 What are decodable texts and how do I identify good ones?

2.7 How should I use decodable texts? When and how should I transition kids out of them?

2.8 If I'm not doing guided reading, what's the best way to approach small-group instructional time?

2.9 What should the other students be doing when I am teaching small groups?

2.10 How much time should I spend on phonics? What should my schedule look like?

I keep hearing about the importance of systematic and explicit phonics instruction. What does that mean?

ANSWER In her "Sold a Story" podcast, education reporter Emily Hanford critiques the widely accepted view in education circles that reading is a natural process, meaning students do not need direct instruction in it. Two key beliefs that stem from this view are 1) if teachers create the right environment and simply guide students, reading will happen as a kind of "natural process" (Episode 23), and 2) that phonics should be taught through mini-lessons that only give children what they need at the time they need it. Research has shown repeatedly, however, that systematic, explicit phonics instruction has far better results for students than the responsive approach (Shanahan, 2005).

Systematic Instruction

Systematic phonics instruction means teaching sound-spelling correspondences in a "clearly defined, carefully selected logical instructional sequence" (Honig, Diamond, & Gutlohn, 2018). Holly Lane, author of UFLI Foundations and a professor at the University of Florida, used the analogy of an architect's blueprint to help us better understand systematic phonics instruction. If an architect is working on a project, she begins with a plan, a blueprint. Some tasks must be completed before others, such as pouring the foundation and creating walls before installing a roof. Once the foundation is set and the framing is finished, she can install windows and doors. Systematic phonics instruction works like that blueprint. It gives you a clear plan for when to introduce specific letter-sound correspondences to students, add new skills to existing ones, and arrange tasks from simplest to most complex (Episode 159).

> "There's no evidence that teaching something explicitly kills a love of that thing.... It's very hard to love doing anything that you can't do."
>
> **—PAMELA SNOW, EPISODE 145**

Explicit Instruction

Explicit instruction is clear, direct, and unambiguous. Concepts are clearly explained, and skills are clearly modeled. Explicit instruction does not require students to discover or infer. During an explicit phonics lesson, you show students a letter, name it, form it, articulate a sound associated with it, and perhaps show its placement in a typical word. Then you explicitly show students how to blend and decode words containing that letter with other letters students have learned and to segment words to encode, or spell, words containing that letter. In addition, you make sure that you are always clear about expectations and continually assess students to ensure they are grasping concepts (Episode 159; Honig, Diamond, & Gutlohn, 2018; Moats & Tolman, 2019).

WHAT YOU CAN DO Literacy researcher Tim Shanahan says, "It is a good idea to use some type of phonics curriculum or program to guide phonics teaching" (2005). Brandon White, UnboundEd ELA Specialist and podcast host, confirms that aligned curriculum is one step to try to make sure that all students are going to be exposed to a certain bar of rigor and content (Episode 79).

So how do you know which programs are best? We recommend The Reading League's Curriculum Evaluation Guidelines (2023) to help answer that question. These guidelines are designed to help a team evaluate curricula to see if they align with evidence of how children learn to read and to identify any non-aligned practices within the curriculum. Section 1: "Word Recognition" contains a detailed checklist of what to look for in an explicit, systematic phonics program.

thereadingleague.org/curriculum-evaluation-guidelines/

CHECK OUT OUR PODCAST, EPISODE 159

"Science of Reading or Snake Oil" with Holly Lane
In this episode, Holly Lane talks to us about the science of reading, as well as research- and evidence-based approaches to teaching literacy. She also explains what the terms *explicit* and *systematic* really mean.

RELATED EPISODES
- **Episode 23:** "Emily Hanford Epically Defines the Science of Reading"
- **Episode 75:** "How Do Language Variants Impact Teaching Reading to African American Students?" with Mitchell Brookins
- **Episode 79:** "What Does Equitable ELA Instruction Require?" with Brandon White and Alice Wiggins
- **Episode 145:** "Debunking Balanced Literacy Arguments" with Pamela Snow

Phonics Scope-and-Sequence Charts

Here is one piece of advice: Do not try to write your own phonics curriculum! It will take too much of your time, and there are many great ones out there already. Some of them are very affordable or even free. Also, keep in mind that the curriculum should be adopted at the school level. You want to be sure that students are learning the same thing across classrooms at each grade level and first- and second-grade teachers know what was taught in previous grades. Here are two examples of a K–2 scope and sequence from UFLI Foundations and Scholastic Ready4Reading (Lane & Contesse, 2022).

Download the "Phonics Scope-and-Sequence" charts.

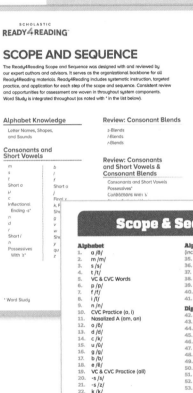

What is orthographic mapping? I'm not sure I understand what that term means.

ANSWER Authors Louisa Moats and Carol Tolman (2019) define orthographic mapping as "the mental process used to store words for immediate and effortless retrieval"—or what happens in the brain that allows us to read words automatically. Reading researcher Linnea Ehri coined the term "orthographic mapping" to describe how people continue developing a bank of words they know by sight as they read. To read text fluently, we must be able to "retrieve words from memory automatically by sight without analyzing letter by letter to decode them" (Miles & Ehri, 2019).

Did you know that our brains are not wired for reading the way they are for speech and vision? So what happens in our brains when we map words? First, we connect the visual form of the word—the letters and letter combinations—with the sounds of the word. We retune the visual part of the brain by mapping those letters and letter combinations to their sounds, and it "glues" the spelling and pronunciation of the word (Episodes 152, 164, and 165).

Then we connect that abstract word to a familiar concept to arrive at the meaning of the word. Claude Goldenberg, author and professor emeritus at Stanford University, told us, "You can teach someone to connect the phonology [pronunciation] with the orthography [spelling], to basically memorize it, but until you can bind that to the semantics [meaning], you can't do what's called orthographic mapping" (Episode 152).

By connecting these three primary areas of the brain—visual, speech, and language—with meaning making, we actually build a new circuit for reading. Isn't that amazing? Ehri (2013) says that orthographic mapping bonds the spellings, pronunciations, and meanings of specific words in our long-term memory.

To secure words in memory, we need multiple exposures to them (Colenbrander et al., 2020). For some of us, it may take only a few exposures before a word is stored in our memory, and we can read it automatically by sight; for others, it takes many more exposures. Also, some foundational skills are needed to facilitate the orthographic mapping process, including knowledge of the relationship between letters and sounds; phonemic awareness, especially segmentation and blending; and letter names and letter sounds (Miles & Ehri, 2019).

WHAT YOU CAN DO You can't "teach" orthographic mapping because it is a mental process, but you can spur that process by giving students plenty of opportunities to decode words. Literacy expert and consultant Shanita Rapatalo asserts that when we teach kids to focus on letters and sounds, we increase activity in areas of the brain that are responsible for reading, and when students memorize words, they're not activating those areas. She says, "You can't memorize every word, and you also can't continue to just guess" (Episode 51).

> "You can teach someone to connect the phonology [pronunciation] with the orthography [spelling] to basically memorize it, but until you can bind that to the semantics [meaning], you can't do what's called orthographic mapping."
>
> **—CLAUDE GOLDENBERG, EPISODE 152**

Julia Lindsey says that decoding is the best strategy for helping students store a word's spelling, pronunciation, and meaning in their long-term memory. In order to decode a word, students must use what they know about the letters and sounds to think about the word's pronunciation (2022). When students decode, they translate printed text into speech by matching graphemes to their corresponding phonemes. Then students must recognize that the patterns make words, and then they can attach meaning to those words.

Have you ever worked with a student who is decoding slowly? We know that it is tempting to jump in and help them out, but if they are beginning readers, let them keep trying. When students are learning to decode, productive struggle is critical because it is how they start to map the words. To get students to store those words in their long-term memory, you will want to give them more repetitions with the same words and similar sound-spelling patterns to help them become automatic and fluent readers.

CHECK OUT OUR PODCAST, EPISODE 164

"Misconceptions About Learning to Read" with Carolyn Strom In this episode, early literacy expert Carolyn Strom discusses that unlike speech, reading doesn't come naturally, and requires well-structured, explicit instruction. She clears up several misconceptions about how the brain learns to read.

RELATED EPISODES

- **Episode 51:** "Science of Reading: An Equity Issue" with Shanita Rapatalo
- **Episode 152:** "Science of Reading for ALL Students: Multilingual Learners" with Claude Goldenberg
- **Episode 165:** "How Brains Learn to Read and Dyslexia" with Nadine Gaab

Your Brain on Reading Graphic

Elise Lovejoy (2023), decodable text author, created this graphic that shows the various parts of the brain involved in orthographic mapping. So what is happening in the brain when we map words? The temporal lobe does a lot of the sound and language processing, as well as connecting words to their meaning. The brain's left side contains areas (parietal and occipital lobe) that are responsible for connecting the sounds with the letters, or graphemes. Then we have an area in the back of the brain, sometimes called the letterbox, where the mapping of oral language onto the print and recognizing that print come together. Then there is the frontal lobe, which is responsible for input and output of speech sounds (Episode 165).

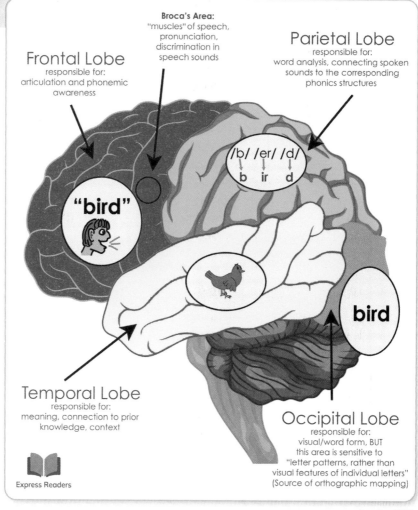

(Lovejoy, 2023)

What is the difference between sight words and high-frequency words?

ANSWER The terms "sight words" and "high-frequency words" are often used interchangeably, and that can be confusing. So let's talk about them individually.

Sight Words

The term sight words has been evolving, at least for some people. Claude Goldenberg told us that the term was once used to describe words that are so phonetically irregular that they can't be decoded, which meant you had to learn them "by sight," or just memorize them as a "big blob." We teachers used to have students read words on flashcards, write words repeatedly, or even memorize them by shape, but the brain is not able to store many words using those methods (Episode 152).

> "A sight word is any word that you can read effortlessly and automatically, without sounding it out or guessing."
>
> **—HEIDI JANE, EPISODE 102**

More current thinking defines sight words as any words that can be read instantly by sight because they have been orthographicallly mapped, which is how our brains can store tens of thousands of words. (See Question 2.2 for more about orthographic mapping.) Any word can become a sight word once a student can read it instantly. Author Jan Wasowicz coined the expression, "Every word wants to be a sight word when it grows up" (Stollar, 2020). Building a large bank of sight words helps students read automatically and fluently.

High-Frequency Words

High-frequency words are words that occur most frequently in print. You may be familiar with lists, such as the Dolch word list (1936) or Fry list (1957), which include the most frequent words in children's books at the time those lists were published.

It's important for students to learn these words early because even the simplest books frequently use words such as *and*, *the*, and *or*. High-frequency words need to become sight words so students can automatically recognize these words in print. How do high-frequency words become sight words if we don't have students memorize them? If they're regular words, students can decode them. Teach them the same way you teach students to decode any word. No need to memorize. If they are irregular words, that's where heart words come in. (Read more about heart words in Question 2.4.)

WHAT YOU CAN DO Julia Lindsey (2022) suggests simultaneously teaching several high-frequency words with similar sound-spelling patterns. For example, if students have only learned that the letter *s* represents the sound /s/, words such as *is*, *has*, and *his* will confuse them because in these words, *s* represents the /z/ sound. Instead of telling students that each of these words is an exception, teach them that another sound *s* can represent is /z/, show them examples, and have them practice decoding and encoding some of these words (Episodes 70 and 71).

Keep in mind that you might need to have students memorize just a few irregular, high-frequency words, such as *the*, *of*, and *you*, especially in early kindergarten, when students are learning the most common sound-spelling correspondences. Research shows that this can be an effective practice for some words, just not for the thousands of words we want students to read automatically (Colenbrander et al., 2020).

To sum up, keep the focus on sound-spelling correspondences as often as possible and keep memorizing to a minimum.

CHECK OUT OUR PODCAST, EPISODE 188

"How to Teach Students to Read Irregular Words"
with Danielle Colenbrander & Katie Pace Miles

Danielle Colenbrander and Katie Pace Miles discuss orthographic mapping, irregular word instruction, and the different terms used to describe high-frequency and irregular words. They provide insights from their research about the effectiveness of different teaching approaches.

RELATED EPISODES

- **Episodes 70 and 71:** "Science of Reading: Decodable Texts, Sound Walls, & the Aim of Early Literacy, Parts 1 and 2," with Julia Lindsey
- **Episode 152:** "Science of Reading for ALL Students: Multilingual Learners" with Claude Goldenberg

TEACHING TOOL

Decodable High-Frequency Words Chart

This chart, from Wiley Blevins's *From Phonics A–Z: A Practical Guide* (2023), lists high-frequency words by phonics skill. The first column contains simple words that students will likely start learning in kindergarten, while the second and third columns contain more complex words that they'll learn later. Use the chart to choose words for instruction. For example, if you are teaching the word *out* and how the first two letters make the /ou/ sound, use the chart to find other words to teach, such as *found* and *round*.

Decodable High-Frequency Words

Phonics Skill	Simple Words (K–1; vowel spelling and single consonants)	Complex Words (1–2; vowel spelling and blends and digraphs)	Multisyllabic Words (2–3; multisyllabic words)
Short *a*	am an as at can had has man ran	and ask back black fast than that	after
Short *e*	get let red ten yes	best help tell them then well went when	better even every myself never open seven yellow
Short *i*	big did him his if in is it sit six	bring drink its pick things think this which will wish with	different into little
Short *o*	got hot not on	long off stop	upon
Short *u*	but cut run up us	jump just much must such	funny number under upon
s-blends		best fast first must stop	

Download "Decodable High-Frequency Words" chart.

What are heart words? How do I teach them?

ANSWER You've probably heard a lot about heart words lately! Heart words are typically high-frequency words that contain irregular parts.

Some high-frequency words can be regularly spelled, such as *up*, *did*, and *him*, and can be decoded with the most common letter sounds. Therefore, they are not heart words.

High-frequency words can also be irregularly spelled, such as *said*, *does*, and *was*. Some of the letters represent the most common phoneme-grapheme correspondence, while others do not. For instance, in the word *was*:

- *w* represents the most common sound for the letter: /w/
- *a* represents the sound /ŭ/, which is at least temporarily irregular for many students
- *s* represents the sound /z/, which is also temporarily irregular for younger children

> "I'm not using *in* or *it* as heart words because my students know how to sound them out. But I taught today that *s* does not say /s/ in *is*, it sounds like /z/. So it is a heart word."
>
> **—KATE WINN, EPISODE 87**

When teaching heart words, guide students to identify parts of the word that they can decode easily, and then focus on irregularly spelled parts that might be tricky to decode. Although there are not currently any studies on using heart words, research shows that students benefit from processing the sound-spelling correspondences of irregular words (Colenbrander et al., 2022).

Why are they called heart words? Because you place a heart under or over the irregularly spelled parts of the word to draw students' attention to that unfamiliar letter-sound correspondence. For instance, for the word *was*, you place a heart under *a* and *s* to show that those letters represent a different sound from what they have learned.

In *Proust and the Squid*, Maryanne Wolf (2007) says, "Luckily, there are fewer irregularly spelled words than is commonly thought, if you are aware of English rules." As an example, the letter *s* represents the sound /z/ 43 percent of the time in the English language. We want to teach this sound-spelling pattern to students, so it is no longer "irregular" (Episode 187). Irregular words are no longer heart words once students have learned the sound-spelling correspondences of them. As with all words, the goal is for heart words to become sight words (Episodes 70, 71, 102, 152, and 164).

WHAT YOU CAN DO Here are elementary teacher Heidi Jane's steps for introducing a heart word:

1. Say the word and have students repeat: *has*

2. Model how to segment and say each sound in the word—or have students do it: /h/ /ă/ /z/

3. Ask students how to spell each sound:

   ◆ "What's the first sound?" /h/ "How do you spell /h/?" *h*

   ◆ "What's the middle sound?" /ă/ "How do you spell /ă/?" *a*

   ◆ "What's the last sound?" /z/ "How do we normally spell /z/?" Most will likely answer *z*. Say: "You are right. We normally spell /z/ with a *z*, but in this word there's a tricky part, and we're going to spell /z/ with an *s*. Place a heart under or over the *s*.

4. Have students read the word, spell the word, and say the word again. Spelling helps students learn high-frequency words. This step is super important!

CHECK OUT OUR PODCAST, EPISODE 102

"Heidi Jane Drops Knowledge on Heart Words and So Much More!" In this episode, Heidi Jane explains the importance of knowing letter sounds when students begin decoding and the difference between sight words and heart words, with examples from her teaching.

RELATED EPISODES

- **Episodes 70 and 71:** "Science of Reading: Decodable Texts, Sound Walls, & the Aim of Early Literacy, Parts 1 and 2," with Julia Lindsey
- **Episode 152:** "Science of Reading for ALL Students: Multilingual Learners" with Claude Goldenberg
- **Episode 164:** "Misconceptions About Learning to Read" with Carolyn Strom
- **Episode 187:** "Understanding the Logic of English" with Denise Eide

What is the relationship between spelling and phonics?

ANSWER Spelling and phonics are like two sides of the same coin. Researchers Nicole Patton-Terry and Carol Connor state, "All beginning spellers are faced with the challenge of mapping their speech patterns to print" (2010). Phonics is making connections between spelling patterns and sounds. When students read words, or decode them, they apply their phonics knowledge, meaning everything they know about the sound and spelling relationship. When they spell words, or encode them, they apply their phonics knowledge to build the word (Episodes 96 and 120).

J. Richard Gentry, co-author of *Brain Words*, says that those skills are reciprocal: Phonics and decoding help spelling, and spelling and encoding help decoding (Episode 96). Louisa Moats and Carol Tolman (2019) say that spelling is usually harder for students than decoding because recalling all the letters in a word is more demanding than recognizing them. That's a big reason why, in *Learning to Read and Learning to Spell Are One and the Same, Almost*, Linnea Ehri states, "Poor spellers do not develop into skilled readers" (Perfetti et al., 1997).

> "Spelling is at the very foundation of the reading architecture in the brain."
>
> —RICHARD GENTRY, EPISODE 96

Encouraging young children to attempt the spelling of words based on the sounds they hear supports their learning of phonics (Shanahan, 2005). Richard Gentry told us that when students practice representing each phoneme with a grapheme, which is known as encoding, it bolsters their decoding development. Also, some research suggests that spending more time on practicing encoding might be even more beneficial for reading development than spending more time on decoding practice (Senechal et al., 2023; van Rijthoven et al., 2021; Conrad et al., 2019).

WHAT YOU CAN DO Remember taking spelling tests in elementary school? We do! We would get a list of seemingly random words on Monday and be told to memorize them by Friday for the test. We might do some homework throughout the week such as writing the word multiple times or using them in sentences. Unfortunately, this was not the best method of instruction to support either spelling or reading development.

Instead of those spelling tests, here is a five-step spelling activity from Richard Gentry (Episode 96) to do with your students:

Step 1: Hear It

Say the word and then read aloud a sentence containing it.

- Activates phonemic awareness by having students listen for the sounds in the word
- Activates the meaning of the word in the brain

Step 2: Say It

Ask students to say the word.

- Activates phonemic awareness by having students pronounce each sound in the word

Step 3: Write It

Ask students to write the word.

- Requires students to convert the sounds they hear in the word to spelling

Step 4: Read It

Show the word to students.

- Promotes self-analysis because students compare the conventional spelling of the word to their spelling of it to see how they represented its various sounds

Step 5: Use It

Have students use the word in literacy activities throughout the week. For example, you can ask them to segment the word using Elkonin boxes or have them read decodable passages that contain the word.

- Incorporates the word into your daily instruction

CHECK OUT OUR PODCAST, EPISODE 96

"What About Spelling?" with Richard Gentry In this episode, Richard Gentry tells us all about spelling and how it connects to our speech and language system. Moreover, he supplies teachers with practical, meaningful, science of reading-aligned strategies to teach spelling.

RELATED EPISODES

- **Episode 120:** "Research-Based Routines for Developing Decoding Skills" with Julia Lindsey
- **Episode 158:** "Science of Reading Beyond Phonics: The Ultimate Goal of Reading" with Doug Fisher

Analyzing Spelling Errors Chart

A child's writing can provide a window into their overall literacy development. Doug Fisher, author and professor, recommends looking at student writing for valuable data. For example, looking at spelling informs you of the phonics patterns students have under control and the patterns they don't. The temporary spelling that students use tells you the sound-spelling correspondences they don't understand and may be struggling with as they decode (Episode 158). The chart below helps to understand the types of errors you might see in student writing, and what you can do to help.

ANALYZING SPELLING ERRORS			
Type of Spelling Error	**Examples**	**What Does It Mean?**	**What Can You Do?**
Phonological	*mush* for *much* *rig* for *ring* *spen* for *spin* *set* for *sent*	• Students are not matching the sounds, or phonemes, and the letters, or graphemes, correctly. • Students may not hear all the sounds in a word correctly. • Students may be producing the phonemes using an English language variant or a different home language.	• Continue explicit instruction on phonemic awareness. • Segment words to ensure students are hearing all the sounds in a word. • Use mirrors to help students see how to make different sounds.
Orthographic	*skool* for *school* *pik* for *pick* *rede* for *ready* *throte* for *throat*	• Students are correctly identifying all the sounds in a word, but they do not know the phoneme-grapheme correspondence for the spelling of the word.	• Explicitly teach additional phoneme-grapheme correspondences that represent a sound (e.g., /k/ can be spelled with *k*, *ck*, *ch*, etc.).
Morphological	*washt* for *washed* *hatz* for *hats* *faver* for *favor* *moshun* for *motion*	• Students are incorrectly spelling meaningful parts of words, or morphemes.	• Focus instruction on morphemes, including prefixes, roots, suffixes, word origins, etc. • Introduce and practice spelling, pronunciation, and meaning of common morphemes.

Download the "Analyzing Spelling Errors" chart.

(Adapted from Literacy Through Language)

What are decodable texts and how do I identify good ones?

ANSWER Decodable texts provide opportunities for students to practice decoding sound-spelling patterns that have been explicitly taught. For example, after you teach a long *e* sound-spelling pattern (e.g., *ea*), you would have students read decodable texts that contain words with that pattern (e.g., *seat*, *meal*) for practice and reinforcement. In short, you give students a chance to apply what you've taught (Episodes 63 and 132).

Students can read the text by directly applying phonics knowledge they have (Episodes 132 and 164). As students repeatedly practice decoding words, they build their bank of sight words. When they read decodable texts, they improve their accuracy, fluency, comprehension, and confidence (Episodes 132, 133, and 134). A joyful milestone to celebrate!

There are more decodable texts available every day, and it can be daunting to know which ones are good and which ones are not.

Quality decodable texts are written according to a solid scope and sequence and capture specific phonics skills that have been introduced. For example, if students are currently learning the most common sound-spelling pattern for short *u* and have already learned sound-spelling patterns for short *a*, *i*, and *o*, the decodable book can and should contain words with the short vowels *a*, *i*, *o*, and *u*. You might see words such as *hat*, *tad*, *fit*, *rip*, *hop*, *sob*, *bug*, and *hut*. But you won't see the words *hike* or *cute*, because those words contain sound-spelling patterns that haven't been taught. Also, quality decodable texts contain few irregular words, or words that students cannot yet decode, such as *here* and *said*.

> "Decodable texts provide purposeful practice."
>
> —KRISTIN POPPENS, EPISODE 63

Decodable texts also contain vocabulary words that pack a punch. For example, students might explore multiple meanings of the word *fit*. Although not the main purpose, decodable texts can be used for basic comprehension when they contain cohesive storylines, facts, and/or text features (Episodes 120, 132, and 133).

Elise Lovejoy tells us that students should be able to decode "the majority of the words," although there isn't an exact percentage that makes a book decodable or not decodable (Episodes 132 and 133). That's not to say that students won't make mistakes reading decodable books. Of course they will—that's part of learning! But quality decodable texts are written for students to succeed.

WHAT YOU CAN DO With quality decodable texts, you take an active role in building students' reading skills and confidence. Take these steps:

1. Teach phonics skills explicitly and systematically.
2. Align quality decodable texts to your phonics scope and sequence.
3. Provide practice opportunities for sound-spelling patterns and high-frequency words you've taught, using those texts (Episode 132).

There are many reliable sources for quality texts, including the Reading League and the Decodable Book Alliance. Some organizations, such as Beyond Decodables, TextProject, and UFLI, offer free decodables, while others offer affordable ones for purchase, including Express Readers, Scholastic, and PhonicBooks.

It's a chimp and a chimp. Chimps can be chums!

A chimp can stand on 2 legs. But it runs on 4 limbs.

CHECK OUT OUR PODCAST, EPISODE 133

"Quality Decodable Texts" with Elise Lovejoy In this episode, decodable book author Elise Lovejoy explains the purpose of decodable texts and how to use them in the classroom.

RELATED EPISODES

- **Episode 63:** "Kindergarten Teacher Reaches 100% Success Using Evidence-Based Practices" with Kristin Poppens
- **Episode 120:** "Research-Based Routines for Developing Decoding Skills" with Julia Lindsey
- **Episode 132:** "The Research on Decodable Text" with Heidi Anne Mesmer
- **Episode 134:** "Small Group Instructional Time" with April Evans
- **Episode 164:** "Misconceptions about Learning to Read" with Carolyn Strom

How should I use decodable texts? When and how should I transition kids out of them?

ANSWER Use decodable texts to support students in practicing phonics skills and high-frequency words you've taught explicitly and systematically, and in connecting words to their meanings (Episode 132). This practice can and should happen in whole-class instruction, small-group instruction, and even at home (Shanahan, 2018). Ernest "Tre" Hadrick III, an educator and a leader, told us a story about how he put decodable texts in the local barber shop (Episode 93)!

Consider aligning decodable texts with current topics of study. For example, if you are studying the changing seasons in science, locate decodable book sets about seasons, trees, hibernation, and so forth, and use them to build content knowledge and reinforce phonics skills (Episodes 134 and 140).

When thinking about which decodable books are right for your students, observe your students reading them. Ask yourself if students are having difficulty or success. Once you've answered that, dig in a bit more. Which students are struggling? Which students aren't? If students are having a difficult time decoding and reading fluently, try giving them texts that are more decodable. If students are successful, give them texts that are less decodable (Shanahan, 2019). Be sure to connect decoding to word meanings for students so they can orthographically map the words.

When students have moved along the continuum, from struggling and reading more-decodable texts to successful and reading less-decodable texts, as well as gaining meaningful vocabulary, it's time to begin transitioning them to authentic trade books.

Literacy experts Linda Farrell and Michael Hunter (2021) recommend moving students into trade books when they can:

1. Accurately read real and nonsense CVC, CCVC, and CVCC words.
2. Decode two-syllable real words (e.g., *until*, *edit*) and familiar three-syllable words (e.g., *inhabit*, *magnetic*) in isolation containing short-vowel syllables.
3. Decode one- and two-syllable real words with *r*-controlled vowels (e.g., *short*, *party*) and silent *e* (e.g., *hope*, *reptile*).

WHAT YOU CAN DO After teaching a phonics skill to the whole class, have all students practice that skill for accuracy. Then based on their performance, support them by continuing accuracy practice or offering opportunities to read fluently and asking comprehension questions (Episodes 92, 133, and 140).

> "Focus on accuracy as the number one priority, then fluency and comprehension."
>
> **—APRIL EVANS, EPISODE 134**

Instructional coach Erin Metz from Blount County, Tennessee, uses assessment and observational data to help students overcome the following hurdles when reading decodable texts.

Hurdle 1: Accuracy and Automaticity of Individual Words

- Have students read decodable texts that contain previously taught sound-spelling patterns and high-frequency words through independent, echo, choral, or buddy reading. (See Question 3.3 for more information.)
- Connect decoding skills to meaning by modeling and practicing unknown words, high-frequency words, or vocabulary words.
- Teach students how to tackle unknown words.

Hurdle 2: Fluency of Phrases

- Build automaticity through repeated readings of decodable texts.
- Teach and have students practice scooping. (See Question 3.2 for details.)
- Practice and model reading small chunks of text.

Hurdle 3: Comprehension

- Emphasize the text's essential understandings.
- If using information-rich decodable books, focus on vocabulary and knowledge-building.
- Teach and have students practice vocabulary and comprehension strategies to make meaning.

 CHECK OUT OUR PODCAST, EPISODE 132

"The Research on Decodable Text" with Heidi Anne Mesmer In this episode, researcher Heidi Anne Mesmer discusses the research on decodable texts, as well as dos and don'ts for classroom practice.

RELATED EPISODES

- **Episode 92:** "Talking About the Elementary Literacy Block with Two Primary Teachers" with April Evans and Danielle Hunter
- **Episode 93:** "School Counselor and Reading Advocate Dad" with Ernest "Tre" Hadrick III
- **Episode 133:** "Quality Decodable Texts" with Elise Lovejoy
- **Episode 140:** "K–2 Literacy Block Deep Dive" with Erin Metz

TEACHING TOOL

Decodable Text Lesson Plan

Our friends at Scholastic shared a lesson plan to help us better understand how to use decodable texts for instruction. The plan includes decodable words with the targeted sound-spelling, the targeted sound-spelling correspondence, a new high-frequency word, and content words. It also includes guidelines for instruction during first and second reads, as well as questions to ask after reading to check comprehension and activities to build writing skills.

Cubs can run in the sun.
Cubs can be pals.
And cubs can play.

Cubs can run and play.
But cubs can get sleepy.
And cubs can nap.
It is fun to look at cubs!

CARD 23
FACT BOOK PAGES

Cub Fun!

Informational Text Type:
Fact Book Pages
A fact book is a text that gives facts and information about a subject.

Summary: These pages from a fact book show photos of polar bear, brown bear, lion, and tiger cubs. The text describes things they can do.

Phonics Focus
• short-u sound /u/ spelled u

Decodable Words with Targeted Sound-Spelling
• cubs
• mud
• run, fun, sun
• tug

New High-Frequency Word
• be

Content Words
• snow, sleepy

Phonemic Awareness and Sound-Spellings Reviews
• /k/ spelled c
• /f/ spelled f

Ask children to listen for and say the first sound of each of these words. Read each word to the children.

• can cat cub car cap
• fun fish fin four five

Then read each row again. Invite children to say the letter that corresponds to the first sound of each word.

MLs Note: See page 7 for ways to leverage children's home language.

Revisit Alphabet Knowledge

Connect Sound-Spelling: /u/ spelled *u*

Remind children that the letter *u* makes the /u/ sound that begins the word *umbrella*. Point out that this short-*u* sound is also found in the middle of words. Write the word *cub* for children and have a volunteer circle the letter *u*.

Then write the word *mud* and have a volunteer circle the letter *u* that makes the /u/ sound in the middle of the word *mud*.

Ask children to suggest other words that have the /u/ sound in the middle. List the words, read them aloud, and have a volunteer circle the letter *u* in each word.

Before Reading

Model Blending Sounds to Make Words

Model for children how to use the /u/ sound to read CVC and VC words. Write the letters *f, u, n* for children. Remind children that the letter *u* makes the /u/ sound that begins *umbrella*. Run your finger under the letters as you slowly blend together the sounds to read the word *fun*, /f/ /u/ /n/. Continue with *up* and *tug*.

Practice Reading Decodable Words

For practice, write the following CVC words for children to read:

sun bus bun run nut tug mud up pup cut bud cub fun

• Have children find the word that rhymes with *bug*. Then have them use their hands and arms to show the meaning of the word *tug*.
• Ask children to find a set of four rhyming words.

Introduce the High-Frequency Word: *be*

Write the high-frequency word *be* in a sentence.

Sam can be fun.

Read aloud the sentence.

• Ask children to find and circle the high-frequency word *be*.
• Help children segment the sounds in *be*, /b/, /ē/. Elicit the letter to write for each sound. For /b/, write *b*; and for /ē/, write *e*. Have children read and spell the word *be*.
• Help children write the word *be*.

First Reading

• Read the title and have children repeat it.
• Read aloud the text, echo-read it, or have children whisper-read on their own.
• Introduce the content word *snow*. Have children look at the picture and tell which animals are in the snow. Have children find the word *snow*. Then ask children to turn over the card and point to the cubs that are sleepy. Then have children find the word *sleepy*.
• Invite children to take turns reading to a partner. Listen to children read and give help as needed.

...nd the Discussion

...and discuss these questions. Encourage children to ...t their thinking with ideas from the text.

...y is it easy for polar bear cubs to hide in the snow?
...at do you think the lion cubs are learning as they play?
...y is it fun to look at cubs and other young animals?

...e From Dictation

...hildren write this sentence. Children may illustrate the ...ce as well. You may want to model the writing.

Mud can be fun.

...e About Reading

...hildren choose one or both of the following options:

...w a picture of each kind of cub. Label the pictures with ...names of the cub. (Informative/Explanatory)
...w a picture that shows which cub you would like to learn ...e about. (Opinion)

Download the "Decodable Text Lesson Plan."

If I'm not doing guided reading, what's the best way to approach small-group instructional time?

ANSWER Differentiated instruction is important. Literacy researcher Julie Washington says, "How we get to teaching with more success with children has to take into account the differences that they bring to reading instruction" (Episode 151). But let's acknowledge a hard truth: There's no evidence for differentiating instruction based on text levels of any kind, including any text leveling system (Episode 143). The term "guided reading" is often synonymous with leveled-reading instruction.

Instead of using levels to group students during small-group instruction, group students by what they need. Target a specific skill to practice, based on a need in decoding, fluency, or comprehension the students have revealed during whole-group instruction (Episode 143; Conradi Smith et al., 2022). You might work with a group of students who have shown a common need for additional practice in a phonics skill you taught to the whole class, such as blending consonants. You might provide direct instruction in the skill, model how to apply it, and give students practice in it. Or you might work with a group of students who are having a difficult time moving from literal meaning to inferential meaning in a text you are reading for ELA.

> "In the review of educational research, we lack research for differentiation by text levels. There's simply no support for that."
>
> **—KRISTIN CONRADI SMITH, EPISODE 143**

We don't need to meet with every student in a small group (Episode 142; Conradi Smith et al., 2022). Authors Kristin Conradi Smith, Steven Amendum, and Tamara Williams believe that small-group instruction is expensive in terms of time, energy, and resources. Think of all the management, prep time, materials, and instructional minutes it takes. What makes small-group instruction worth the cost? It allows us to address the needs of several students through brief, targeted instruction and practice with a narrow focus. It should be as effective and efficient as possible for all students, including the students with whom we're not working. So how can we ensure that? (Episode 143; Conradi Smith et al., 2022).

WHAT YOU CAN DO Plan for small-group time, keeping in mind these "ABCs" from Conradi Smith, Amendum, and Williams (2022):

- **A** = Assessment
- **B** = Basics and Books
- **C** = Clear Directions and Feedback

Assessment

Sort students into flexible, fluid groups based on results from high-quality formative assessments (during instruction) and summative assessments (at the end—or culmination—of instruction).

If most of your students struggle with a concept you've taught, and don't perform well on assessments, reteach it to the whole class. Small-group instruction should not replace whole-group instruction (Shanahan, 2018).

Basics and Books

Small groups are most effective when crafted to meet specific needs of students determined through assessment, otherwise known as "the basics" (Hall & Burns, 2018). Teaching the basics may mean reteaching specific phonemic awareness and phonics skills students need. You might use decodable books to help them develop those skills. Or you might use complex, grade-level texts for making sense of syntax or summarizing key understandings.

Clear Directions and Feedback

Small-group instruction allows you to zoom in on students as they learn. This is a huge benefit to both you and your students, but it needs to be highly strategic and purposeful. You can maximize small-group time by giving clear directions. Also, share success stories, which helps students develop a growth mindset and reflect on big and small accomplishments (Conradi Smith et al., 2022).

 CHECK OUT OUR PODCAST, EPISODE 143

"Maximizing Small-Group Reading Instruction" with Kristin Conradi Smith, Steven Amendum, and Tamara Williams In this episode, we talk about the research on small-group time and what we know about effective use of that time. The guests help us understand constrained skills and unconstrained skills, and when and how to best teach them.

RELATED EPISODES

- **Episode 142:** "Structured Literacy in Small-Group Time" with Casey Jergens and Natalie Wexler
- **Episode 151:** "Science of Reading for ALL Students: Language Variation and Reading" with Julie Washington

What should the other students be doing when I am teaching small groups?

ANSWER

Casey Jergens, a kindergarten teacher from Minneapolis, Minnesota, shifted his approach to small groups after spending lots of time, money, and energy on centers and realizing that students were not necessarily using them as intended. Instead, he learned how to make the most of this time for all students, particularly those engaged without his direct guidance (Episode 142).

First, use small-group instruction time sparingly and with intention—for example, as a time to work on skills for which certain students need additional practice.

Second, if there are other qualified adults in your classroom, recruit them to help students you're not working with.

Third, consider grouping students with similar needs across classrooms. For example, you might send students who need more practice with blending and segmenting to another classroom for additional practice with those skills. This reduces the number of students working without you (Episode 142; Diamond, 2023).

However, we should note that the most effective time spent in school is with the teacher. So to maximize the amount of time students spend with you, think about how to minimize independent work time. Often classrooms become too noisy while students are at centers or stations, even with the best-set expectations (Episode 142; Wexler, 2022). But there is a place for small-group instruction if it's well-implemented. (See Question 2.8 for ideas.)

WHAT YOU CAN DO Keep. It. Simple. Yup, simple! When students are working without you, they should be reviewing and practicing what you've taught, rather than learning anything new (Episode 80). Here are big questions to ask yourself as you plan:

1. What skills have I taught that students can practice independently?
2. What instructional routines have I taught that students can follow?
3. How can students connect skills and routines to content or topics they are learning?

Ways to review skills. Have students:

- play phonics games, such as letter-sound bingo, to review sound-spelling patterns.
- create word ladders. (For more information on word ladders, see Question 1.7.)
- use Rime Mats to blend phonemes to decode words. (For more information on Rime Mats, see Question 1.5.)

Ways to review instructional routines. Have students:

- partner-read short chunks of grade-level texts for fluency practice.
- reread decodable texts, focusing on accuracy and fluency.
- explore vocabulary terms during pre-taught routines, such as those suggested in Question 4.10.

Ways to review content and topics. Have students:

- watch brief videos with closed captioning and take notes.
- listen to audiobooks or kids' podcasts (Episode 80).
- review vocabulary through repeated use of terms in writing and fluency practice.
- read books, articles, poems, and other texts to build content knowledge for ELA, science, social studies, and other subjects.

 CHECK OUT OUR PODCAST, EPISODE 142

"Structured Literacy in Small-Group Time" with Casey Jergens and Natalie Wexler In this episode, we discuss the structure and content of the literacy block. What does structured literacy look like in small groups?

RELATED EPISODES

- **Episode 80:** "A Primary Teacher's Perspective on Science of Reading, Small-Group Instruction, and Sound Walls" with Lindsay Kemeny
- **Episode 143:** "Maximizing Small-Group Reading Instruction" with Kristin Conradi Smith, Steven Amendum, and Tamara Williams

How much time should I spend on phonics? What should my schedule look like?

ANSWER Time is always on teachers' minds! For K–2, we mostly see literacy blocks ranging from 90 to 120 minutes. Within the block, teachers usually dedicate time to foundational skills in both whole-group and small-group instruction and have time dedicated to language comprehension. In upper grades, the time for language comprehension increases and time dedicated to foundational skills decreases.

Whole-group foundational skills time ranges from 20 to 45 minutes, with 30 minutes being the most common. This is time to build phonemic awareness, decoding, encoding, and fluency skills. Casey Jergens reminds us that lengthier whole-group instruction does not mean students are sitting passively and listening to the teacher: "We're switching it up every five to six minutes throughout those blocks of time. It's very engaging and interactive, but I am with the kids all the time" (Episode 142).

The focus of small-group instruction is often foundational skills but can extend to vocabulary and comprehension. Small-group instruction ranges from 15 to 45 minutes and is usually around 30 minutes. Differentiated small-group instruction is a part of nearly all literacy blocks because of the varied needs of students that can best be addressed more effectively when the teacher, in the moment, is responsible for fewer students (Conradi Smith et al., 2022). (See Question 2.8 for more information on small-group instruction.)

The rest of the literacy block is typically around 60 minutes and focuses on language comprehension to build oral language, background knowledge, and vocabulary. In primary grades, this time is typically spent on read-alouds of complex texts with discussion and writing to help students comprehend the text. Once students can read independently, you can allow students to do more reading on their own during this time and focus on reading comprehension (Episodes 134, 140, and 142).

> "If you're thinking about a two-hour literacy block, about half of the time is devoted to foundational literacy, and then about half of the time to content literacy. And most of that time is done whole group."
>
> —CASEY JERGENS, EPISODE 142

WHAT YOU CAN DO Repetition and review are critical to phonics instruction, so make sure they are part of your schedule. Extra practice enables students to lock in their skills, or in the case of reading, orthographically map phoneme-grapheme correspondences. (See Question 2.2 for more information about orthographic mapping.)

Holly Lane introduced us to the practice of *interleaving*, which is essential to how you structure your phonics lessons. She explained that after you introduce and have students practice a concept in one lesson, you should move on to a new concept in the next lesson, whether students have mastered that first one or not. However, you need to review the original concept over time. For example, if you introduce the short *i* sound in one lesson, over the next five weeks, be sure students continue to practice hearing the sound, seeing the corresponding graphemes, segmenting and blending words with the sound, decoding words that include the corresponding graphemes, and spelling words that include the letter-sound correspondence, as you introduce them to new phoneme-grapheme correspondences. Over those five weeks, students could see the short *i* sound, and corresponding letter over 300 times. Interleaving leads to long-term retention of a concept and can be a powerful tool for learning to read (Episode 159; Firth et al., 2021).

CHECK OUT OUR PODCAST, EPISODE 140

"K–2 Literacy Block Deep Dive" with Erin Metz In this episode, we talk with instructional coach Erin Metz, and she provides an in-depth walk-through of her district's K–2 instructional block time. She shares her strategic approach to working with students during small-group time, modeling how to use this time to reinforce accuracy and automaticity, and to build vocabulary and knowledge to solidify comprehension and more.

RELATED EPISODES

- **Episode 134:** "Small-Group Instructional Time" with April Evans
- **Episode 142:** "Structured Literacy in Small-Group Time" with Casey Jergens and Natalie Wexler
- **Episode 159:** "Science of Reading or Snake Oil" with Holly Lane

TEACHING TOOL

Components of Whole-Group Phonics Instruction

What should happen during whole-group instruction in phonics? Here are some research-based ideas. Keep in mind, you may want to incorporate some of them in small-group instruction, based on the needs of your students.

WHOLE-GROUP PHONICS INSTRUCTION

Component	Purpose	What to Do
Review	• To give students more repetition, which is helpful for orthographic mapping	• Review previously learned graphemes and have students say phonemes. • Say previously learned sounds. Then have students repeat and form letters (dry-erase board, pencil/paper, finger on carpet, etc.). • Have students create word ladders. (See Question 1.7.)
Phonemic Awareness	• To provide a brief warm-up to the lesson • To review previously learned sounds • To prime students for connecting phonemes to graphemes	• Have students practice isolating, segmenting, and blending. (See Question 1.5.) • Introduce the phoneme first when introducing a new phoneme-grapheme correspondence.

Decoding	• To give students practice sounding out words on their own
	• To allow time and space for productive struggle
		• Have students blend phonemes and read the word.
		• Have students do word work, including word ladders.
		• Introduce new letter-sound correspondences, focusing on:
		  ◆ pronouncing the sound, paying attention to where the sound is formed in the mouth.
		  ◆ forming the letter(s).
		  ◆ guided practice in reading and spelling words.

Spelling	• To practice encoding words • To use as a formative assessment	• Dictate words and sentences. • Have students write words on paper, dry-erase boards, or the rug using a finger. Or have them build words using magnetic letters or letter tiles.
Reading	• To read connected text to apply their knowledge	• Have students read and reread sentences. • Have students read and reread decodable text. • Offer opportunities for fluency practice.
Irregular Word Instruction	• To introduce irregular, high-frequency words	• Use the heart-word method to introduce words. (See Question 2.4.)

Download the "Whole-Group Phonics Instruction" planner.

(Lane & Contesse, 2022; Mesmer, 2019)

CHAPTER 3

FLUENCY

Fluency is the ability to read text with reasonable accuracy, appropriate pacing to allow for comprehension, and suitable expression or prosody so the text sounds meaningful.

MELISSA'S STORY

I remember vividly trying to improve my middle schoolers' fluency by having them use stopwatches to determine how many words per minute they could read aloud. I also remember those good intentions going off the rails! There was nothing my eager and competitive students wanted more than to show me and their classmates just how fast they could read. And they went for it—to the point I could barely make out what they were reading. At the time, I didn't know enough about fluency to tell my students what they should be doing instead of vying for the title of "the fastest reader in Ms. Loftus's class."

Because fluency was not a part of the middle school standards, and "speed reading" wasn't improving my students' reading, I gave up... until I read this statement from the National Reading Panel (2000): "It is generally acknowledged that fluency is a critical component of skilled reading. Nevertheless, it is often neglected in classroom instruction." As I learned more about the importance of fluency, I realized that giving up was not the answer, and finding another way to develop it was.

Children's oral reading fluency has a considerable impact on how they translate speech into print as they learn to read and spell. That's what this chapter is all about. Let's get started!

Questions That Keep You Up at Night

3.1 What is fluency? What makes a fluent reader fluent?

3.2 I've heard that fluency is the bridge between word recognition and comprehension. Why?

3.3 What is the difference between modeled reading, echo reading, choral reading, and partner reading? When should my students and I use each?

3.4 Readers' Theater seems fun and easy to implement. But is it an effective practice, according to research?

3.5 How much time should I spend on fluency? What should my schedule look like?

3.6 How do decodable texts build fluency in early readers?

3.7 I have a student who can sound out words but reads slowly. How do I provide support to increase automaticity?

3.8 I've heard that one-minute oral reading fluency assessments are important. What can I learn from them?

3.9 The oral reading fluency assessment does not measure expression. So what can I use to measure it?

3.10 What kinds of texts should I use for fluency instruction and practice?

What is fluency? What makes a fluent reader fluent?

ANSWER You might hear people say that fluency is reading quickly, but that is a misconception. Although reading speed is a part of fluency, it is more nuanced. Jan Hasbrouck, a fluency researcher, defines fluency as "text read with a reasonable accuracy, appropriate rate, and suitable expression or prosody that represents that you understand what you've read" (Episode 153). Let's take a closer look at those terms.

> "Automaticity has somehow morphed into making kids read fast. We measure automaticity by speed of reading. So, we try to improve reading by getting kids to read faster. And, of course, that doesn't work at all. We end up with fast readers, but not very good readers."
>
> **—TIM RASINSKI, EPISODE 62**

Accuracy

Accuracy means reading the words on the page correctly. For students to make sense of a text, they need to read at least 95 percent of its words accurately, and for younger students, it should be closer to 98 percent (International Literacy Association, 2018). To read accurately, students must have a strong foundation in word recognition.

Rate

Rate, also referred to as pacing, is the speed at which students read. Reading rate depends on students' ability to recognize and read words automatically. (Learn about how students become automatic word readers in Question 2.2.) If students are working hard to decode each word, their reading rate will be slow. But guess what? A fast reader is not necessarily a fluent reader! If students are reading too quickly, they are unlikely to make sense of the text. We want students reading at an appropriate rate, similar to the pace of a conversation (Episode 62). (Read how to assess accuracy and rate in Question 3.8.)

Expression

Expression, also known as prosody, includes chunking words into appropriate phrases, pausing at appropriate points, emphasizing key words, and maintaining a natural tone, volume, and rhythm. The level of expression indicates whether a reader is making sense of the text. (Read how to assess expression in Question 3.9.)

WHAT YOU CAN DO District leader Angie Hanlin explicitly teaches students about accuracy, rate, and expression. The clearer and more transparent you can be with students about what it takes to improve reading, the more you empower them. Here are some quick tips from her (Episode 108):

When you are reading aloud:

- To support accuracy, pause and think aloud about how to decode unfamiliar or multisyllabic words.
- To support rate, always model reading at an appropriate pace—try not to read too quickly or too slowly.
- To support expression, don't be afraid to be dramatic as you read to show students how to read with expression.

When you are listening to students read aloud:

- To support accuracy, pay attention to how many words students read incorrectly, or if they are taking a lot of time to decode words. Think about follow-up assessments that might be needed.
- To support rate, remind students to "read like you talk, not as quickly as you can."
- To support expression, provide specific feedback such as, "Notice the exclamation point at the end. That means the speaker is excited, so you want to read that sentence with excitement in your voice."

> A fluent reader...
> - reads the words correctly
> - reads at a natural speed
> - sounds like they are having a natural conversation
> - reads with expression
> - pays attention to punctuation
> - emphasizes important words or phrases
> - checks their understanding

⏸ CHECK OUT OUR PODCAST, EPISODE 62

"Effective Fluency Instruction" with Tim Rasinski In this episode, fluency expert Tim Rasinski shares why fluency should be hot, and how to support students in all aspects of it, including accuracy, rate, and expression.

RELATED EPISODES

- **Episode 153:** "Science of Reading Beyond Phonics: Fluency Instruction and Assessment" with Jan Hasbrouck
- **Episode 154:** "Science of Reading Beyond Phonics: Fluency Instructional Routines" with Nathaniel Swain

I've heard that fluency is the bridge between word recognition and comprehension. Why?

ANSWER Fluency is often referred to as the bridge between phonics and comprehension, and we can see why! Meredith Liben and Sue Pimentel, authors of "Placing Text at the Center of the Standards-Aligned ELA Classroom," state that "dysfluency causes as much as 40 percent of the variance in students who pass tests versus those who fail" (2018). Assessment results of reading fluency are strong predictors of success in reading comprehension. In fact, some studies have shown that oral reading fluency is the strongest predictor (Honig, Diamond, & Gutlohn, 2018; Wise et al., 2010).

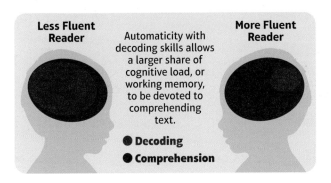

So why is there a correlation between fluency and comprehension? Readers have a finite amount of attention to use while reading (Sweller, 1988). Tim Rasinski says the goal of phonics instruction is to get kids not using phonics (Episode 62). If they devote too much attention to decoding, they do not have enough cognitive energy to make meaning of individual words and whole texts. When they recognize words automatically, and make meaning as they read, they can comprehend.

Tim compares reading to driving a car. Remember when you first learned to drive and had to devote all your attention to which pedal to use? You probably had to turn off the radio when you were parking so you could focus. But as you practiced driving, you became more accurate and automatic, which meant you didn't have to think about every move. That's what it's like for students who are just learning to decode. Most of their attention is on decoding. But ideally, they get to the point of reading accurately and automatically, and can pay attention to the text's meaning (Episode 62).

Expression is also critical to students' comprehension. According to authors David Liben and David Paige, "Students who read with prosody are more likely to understand what they read" (2016). Students make more sense of the text when they read with expression, and read with more expression when they make sense of the text.

WHAT YOU CAN DO You can help students understand what they are reading by encouraging them to read in meaningful phrases: "Good readers make meaning by reading in phrases; struggling readers limit meaning by reading word by word" (Rasinski, Ellery, & Oczkus, 2015). Here are a few ideas to try:

Phrasing

Give students a text marked with slashes to indicate pauses: one slash for a short pause at the end of a meaningful phrase or when there is a comma, and two slashes for a longer pause at the end of a sentence. See the next page for an example.

Scooping

Draw curved lines underneath meaningful groups of words and have students "scoop them up" as they read. See the next page for an example.

Depending on your students' needs, provide the slashes or scoops for them. Read the text aloud as students follow along, choral-read, or echo-read, or let students practice on their own by whisper-reading or reading to a partner.

For more challenge, let students decide where the slashes or scoops would go before they practice reading the text on their own. After they have practiced reading the marked text, give the students a clean copy and have them practice reading in meaningful phrases again.

> "Reading fluency is obviously very affected by your word recognition, but it's also affected by your language comprehension and affects your language comprehension."
>
> **—NELL DUKE, EPISODE 66**

CHECK OUT OUR PODCAST, EPISODE 66

"Re-thinking the Reading Rope" with Nell Duke
Nell Duke talks all about the science of reading comprehension, including the role of fluency, in this episode.

RELATED EPISODES

- **Episode 62:** "Effective Fluency Instruction" with Tim Rasinski
- **Episode 153:** "Science of Reading Beyond Phonics: Fluency Instruction and Assessment" with Jan Hasbrouck
- **Episode 154:** "Science of Reading Beyond Phonics: Fluency Instructional Routines" with Nathaniel Swain

TEACHING TOOL

Marked Texts for Fluency Practice

Before asking students to phrase or scoop texts, MODEL, MODEL, MODEL! It is important for students to see how you would break up a text and hear you read the text aloud with pauses. You can also show students what NOT to do. For instance, you can put a slash after every word and then talk about how choppy that sounds, or you can end a scoop where it would sound awkward to stop (e.g., "The Amazon rainforest in"). Just make sure that students are clear that these are incorrect and talk about why they are.

Phrasing: Chunking words together into meaningful phrases

The Amazon rainforest / in South America /

is very big. //

If it was a country, /

it would be the ninth biggest / in the world.

Scooping: Grouping words together into meaningful phrases

The Amazon rainforest   in South America

is very big.

If it was a country,

it would be the ninth biggest   in the world.

What is the difference between modeled reading, echo reading, choral reading, and partner reading? When should my students and I use each?

ANSWER David and Meredith Liben, authors of *Know Better, Do Better* (2019), tell us that the research is clear about how to improve fluency. They say that you want children following along while a skilled reader reads a passage aloud, and you want students doing repeated readings of a passage after hearing fluent reading. Researchers Steven Stahl and Kathleen Heubach (2005) agree that repeated readings are beneficial for improving students' fluency. Let's learn about four concrete ways you can incorporate these findings into your classroom.

Modeled Reading

You read aloud while students track the text or follow along. Listening to you read fluently allows students to hear how to pronounce words accurately and exposes them to appropriate pace and expression.

Echo Reading

You read aloud a short passage, sentence by sentence, to provide a fluent model, and then students immediately echo back what was modeled. Echo reading gives students the opportunity to hear fluent reading and immediately practice it on their own.

Choral Reading

You and students all read the same short passage at the same time. Choral reading allows students to practice reading fluently in the company of others.

Partner Reading

You start by pairing a stronger reader with a reader who's not quite as strong. Then have one student read aloud while the other student tracks in the text. From there, have them switch roles so each student has a turn to hear the text read by their partner and practice reading the text. Partner reading allows you to listen to students as they practice reading fluently and offer feedback.

For all these strategies, students must have clear access to the text so they can see the words as they read.

> "The reason [choral reading] is helpful is because every student is basically supported by one another to follow along with the text, to hear fluent reading whilst they're also producing fluent reading."
>
> —NATHANIEL SWAIN, EPISODE 154

WHAT YOU CAN DO Partner reading improves reading rate, as well as accuracy and comprehension for all students if it is properly organized (Topping, 2014). Primary teacher and author Lindsay Kemeny explains how she makes partner reading successful. Her class went from a median score of 50 words per minute to an ideal rate of 64 words per minute in just two weeks after she implemented a partner-reading routine (Episode 98; Kemeny, 2023).

Look Closely at the Data

Kemeny uses data from her assessments to pair students, so each pair is made up of a student reading on the higher end of the words per minute, and another is at the lower end. She keeps an eye on the data and, based on it, changes partners often. She thinks about students' expression, too. If students are struggling with prosody, she knows hearing classmates read with expression will help.

Teach Students to Coach Each Other

Kemeny teaches her students Anita Archer's simple error-correction protocol. The partner who is not reading aloud follows along with the reader. When she hears her partner say a word incorrectly, she points to it and asks, "Can you figure out this word?" Then she gives her partner four seconds to pronounce the word correctly. If he can't, she says, "This word is ____. What word? Now reread the sentence" (Archer & Hughes, 2011).

	Teacher...	Students...
Modeled Reading	reads aloud a text	follow along in a copy of the text, with a finger or other tool (e.g., a pencil)
Echo Reading	reads aloud short chunks of text	read aloud from a copy of the text, after the teacher reads
Choral Reading	reads aloud a text	read aloud the same text at the same time as the teacher
Partner Reading	listens to students read aloud and provides feedback on accuracy, rate, or expression	take turns reading while the other student follows along in a copy of the text

CHECK OUT OUR PODCAST, EPISODE 154

"Science of Reading Beyond Phonics: Fluency Instructional Routines" with Nathaniel Swain In this episode, Nathaniel Swain, senior lecturer at La Trobe University in Australia, breaks down his top three instructional routines to improve students' fluency, including tracked reading, choral reading, and paired reading, and the research that supports each.

RELATED EPISODE

- **Episode 98:** "Improving Student Reading Growth in Months with Fluency Instruction and Practice" with Lindsay Kemeny and Lorraine Griffith

TEACHING TOOL

Ways to Read Slide

Kory Jensen, a fourth-grade teacher from Aurora, Colorado, uses this slide when students practice fluency in small groups. He and his students read a text multiple times, a different way each time. Check out the chart below to see what he and his students do for each type of reading.

Choral Read

Everyone reads together

Three ways to reread a text with your group.

Pick a different way to read the text EVERY TIME you reread today.

Reading with one person in your group

Buddy Read

Independent Read

Everyone reads by themselves

Readers' Theater seems fun and easy to implement. But is it an effective practice, according to research?

ANSWER Readers' Theater is fun—and it is effective, according to research! Tim Rasinski says that we need to give students opportunities to perform and to be creative with their voices. Readers' Theater is one way to do that.

What is Readers' Theater? Students perform by reading a script aloud. It's sort of like acting, but they do not need to memorize the script or necessarily use costumes or props (although costumes and props can enhance the fun). Before they perform, students repeatedly read the script to practice. Repeated reading "provides the targeted, focused practice needed to improve all areas of reading fluency—accuracy, rate, and prosody—and is one of the most studied methods for increasing reading fluency" (Honig, Diamond, & Gutlohn, 2018). Performing for a real audience gives students an authentic reason to practice reading accurately and at a natural rate. It gives them a purpose for reading with expression (Prescott, 2015).

> "We found out that the [students] really enjoyed the collaborative aspect, the performance aspect, and because the scripts were somewhat humorous, they also liked entertaining their peers...they were successful and they were feeling it."
>
> **—CHASE YOUNG, EPISODE 122**

Researcher and professor, Chase Young, told us about his study of Readers' Theater. The second-grade students in the study practiced their scripts each day for a week before performing it. Reading comprehension improved for all students who participated, but it improved the most for students who tested significantly lower in decoding, vocabulary, and reading comprehension prior to the study. Most interestingly, Chase and his colleagues learned from the students that they didn't think that Readers' Theater could possibly improve their reading because it was too fun (Episode 122; Young, Mohr, & Landreth, 2020).

Neena Saha, from Reading Research Recap, told us about a meta-analysis on the impact of Readers' Theater. After reviewing multiple studies, they found that the technique not only improves students' reading skills, but also helps them to develop a positive attitude toward reading (Episode 160; Mastrothanasis et al., 2023).

WHAT YOU CAN DO Readers' Theater can be a fun addition to your instructional routine—and easy to do:

1. Break the class into small groups.
2. Give each group a script related to something they have read or are studying in class.
3. Assign parts of the script to students and have them practice reading those parts orally.
4. Have students perform the script for an audience.

Most importantly, do not ask students to memorize the script. They should read the script when they perform, as fluently as they possibly can. That's why pre-performance practice is so important.

Readers' Theater scripts may be part of your reading program. If they aren't, you can find them online. We recommend the ones on Chase Young's website (TheBestClass.org) and in the *Fluency Practice Read-Aloud Plays* ebooks from Scholastic. Alternatively, you can create your own scripts or have students create them. Regardless of where scripts come from, they should relate to content or topics you are covering in class.

In addition to Readers' Theater, have students take part in authentic performances that give them a chance to practice reading orally. For example, if students are reading and writing poems for a poetry unit, find a time and place for them to perform those poems for other students or adults in the building, or their families or caregivers. We suspect your students will be so excited, they won't even know they are working on reading fluency.

CHECK OUT OUR PODCAST, EPISODE 122

"Reading as Science AND Art" with Tim Rasinski, David Paige, and Chase Young In this episode, we talk with the authors of *Artfully Teaching the Science of Reading*. We dive into many topics related to teaching reading, including fluency and Readers' Theater.

RELATED EPISODE

- **Episode 160:** "Understanding Reading Research" with Neena Saha

TEACHING TOOL

Readers' Theater Prep Chart and Sample Script

When your students are getting ready for Readers' Theater, share these tips for ensuring a great performance and be sure to choose a script that's fun to read and connects to a topic of study, such as this one on earthquakes.

Top Tips for Readers' Theater

- **Practice, Practice, Practice!** Practice reading your lines, so you are **reddy** to perform.

- **Be Expressive!** Read your character's lines to show how they **feel**.

- **Can We Hear You?** Speak loudly, clearly, and at a natural pace.

"Earthquake!"

CHARACTERS

Rick Terscale
Andreas Fault
Mag Nitude
Moe Shun
Shay King

Rick: Hello, and welcome to the most rockin' game show around: Earthquake! I'm your host, Rick Terscale. Let's meet today's contestants, shall we?

Andreas: I'm Andreas Fault, and I'm a restaurant manager from Cantwell, Alaska.

Mag: I'm Mag Nitude, and I'm a computer expert from Glen Rock, New Jersey.

Moe: My name is Moe Shun, and I'm a geologist at California State University.

Shay: I'm Shay King, and I run a science camp in Twin Falls, Idaho.

Rick: Okay, contestants, get ready for your first question. For 100 points, please hit your buzzers if you know the answer to: WHAT IS AN EARTHQUAKE?

(Each player hits a buzzer, but only Andreas's buzzer lights up.)

Rick: Okay, Andreas. Please tell us: WHAT IS AN EARTHQUAKE?

76

Fluency Practice Read-Aloud Plays, Grades 3–4 • Scholastic Teaching Resources

Download the sample script.

How much time should I spend on fluency? What should my schedule look like?

ANSWER Students should have time to practice fluency every day—but not a lot of time. Meredith Liben and Sue Pimentel (2018) recommend 15 to 20 minutes, using grade-level texts. You want to think about quick ways to explicitly teach and allow students to practice fluency throughout each day. Brandon White, UnboundEd ELA Specialist, says that the best part of fluency instruction is that "it's really pretty easy to implement. It doesn't take a lot of time" (Episode 79).

It might be helpful to think about what a schedule for fluency looks like over the course of a week because you want to build on what students do each day as they become more familiar and increasingly fluent with the text.

Tim Rasinski shared an example of a weekly routine for a class studying great American poets.

Monday: The teacher assigned one of five different poems by the same poet to each student. She read the poems aloud to the students, while they followed along in their own copies.

Tuesday: She had students read their poems quietly to themselves.

Wednesday: She put students into small groups to read their poems aloud, as she gave feedback.

Thursday: She had students quickly rehearse their poems.

Friday: She had students perform their poems for the principal, parents, or other visitors.

> "Practice, practice, practice, but also perform. Without the performance aspect... [students are] not really seeing a reason for doing it."
>
> **—LORRAINE GRIFFITH, EPISODE 98**

Students got daily fluency practice in an authentic way, and deepened their knowledge of the poet and poetry they were studying (Episode 62).

WHAT YOU CAN DO Think about authentic ways for your students to perform texts during class to make repeated reading purposeful. Lorraine Griffith, Chief Knowledge Officer at Great Minds and former teacher, reminds us of the importance of having students practice whatever we're teaching them. Performance shows them that practice in oral reading pays off.

Lindsay Kemeny says that if you are worried about time (and what teacher is not?), put students into small groups and have them perform within their group. She does not force any student to perform who doesn't want to because it can do more harm than good to students, especially if they are struggling and self-conscious. It might be best to have those students record their performance and share the recording with peers or perform live one-on-one with a trusted adult (Episode 98).

Tanisha Dasmunshi, a middle-school teacher from Baltimore, was worried about having adequate time for fluency instruction. So she made it part of her in-class routine, in a quick, meaningful way. Her students love to perform, and they were particularly excited to perform Squealer's speech from *Animal Farm*. They mastered reading that speech and performing it for their peers. They understood its humor because they were reading and discussing the book in ELA, and they wound up comprehending it at a deeper level due to reading it repeatedly before their performance (Episode 110).

In addition to designating time for repeated reading and performance, think about quick ways to fit in fluency practice throughout the day. You might choral-read the directions to an assignment or echo-read the definition of a new word that you are introducing. This can happen across content areas and does not have to happen only during a time of day focused on fluency.

 CHECK OUT OUR PODCAST, EPISODE 98

"Improving Student Reading Growth in Months with Fluency Instruction and Practice" with Lindsay Kemeny and Lorraine Griffith

We talked with two knowledgeable teacher friends. Lindsay Kemeny shares details of her current fluency routines for second graders, and Lorraine Griffith shares details of her practices from when she was in the classroom.

RELATED EPISODES

- **Episode 62:** "Effective Fluency Instruction" with Tim Rasinski
- **Episode 79:** "What Does Equitable ELA Instruction Require?" with Brandon White and Alice Wiggins
- **Episode 110:** "Baltimore Secondary Literacy Teachers Talk Fluency" with Tanisha Dasmunshi, Emily Jaskowski, and Emery Uwimana

TEACHING TOOL

Repeated Reading Routine

Use a weekly schedule like this to ensure regular fluency practice. Think about how students can benefit from repeated readings of selected sentences or passages, and where and when they can perform texts they've read or written themselves. At the beginning of the week, give students a lot of support through modeled, choral, and echo reading and then let them practice more independently toward the end of the week.

REPEATED READING ROUTINE SAMPLE WEEKLY SCHEDULE

Monday	Tuesday	Wednesday	Thursday	Friday
Teacher reads a longer passage aloud to students. Teacher and students choral-read a shorter portion of the text. Students practice reading on their own by whisper-reading.	Teacher reads aloud the shorter portion of the text. Teacher and students echo-read the text. Students practice reading on their own by whisper-reading.	Students practice reading the text aloud with a partner. Teacher listens and provides feedback to students.	Students rehearse for their performance using a checklist to self-evaluate.	Students perform or record reading the text aloud.

Download the "Repeated Reading Routine Sample Weekly Schedule."

(Adapted from Student Achievement Partners Weekly Reading Practice Routine)

How do decodable texts build fluency in early readers?

ANSWER Decodable texts are simple books written specifically for students who are just learning to read. They give students a chance to use their phonemic awareness and phonics skills to decode words. Practice with decodable texts helps students become accurate and automatic readers—in other words, fluent readers. However, the components of fluency—accuracy, rate, and expression—do not develop at the same time and decodable texts have an important role in the early stages.

When students are learning to decode, you do not need to focus on rate and expression. Instead, focus on accuracy. It's critical to give students opportunities to read texts that contain words with phonics patterns you've taught. This is what decodable texts are for (Episodes 91 and 98)! They give students opportunities to decode those words accurately by connecting the visual form of the letters and words to the sounds. (Read more about decodable texts in Questions 2.6 and 2.7.)

> "You just want to do phonics really well, really early, so that we get students moving towards automatic word recognition and fluent reading as quickly and as easily as possible."
>
> **—NATHANIEL SWAIN, EPISODE 154**

Once students are reading words accurately, they can then start to think about the meaning of those words, or you can help students understand the words if they do not already know them. After several repetitions, those words are stored and can be read automatically. This is called orthographic mapping. Decodable texts can help students orthographically map words and read automatically and independently. (Read more about orthographic mapping in Question 2.2.)

When students read automatically, they can make meaning from those words just as quickly. This is when they can start reading with expression. You may use decodable texts for this type of practice, but it's likely that you will want to start using more authentic texts at this point, too (Episode 164).

WHAT YOU CAN DO After you teach a sound-letter pattern, use decodable texts that contain that pattern (and previously taught patterns) for students to apply the phonics knowledge. This helps them with accuracy and leads to automaticity. Here are some tips from teachers April Evans and Lindsay Kemeny about working with decodable texts during small-group instruction.

- Some groups might be working on CVC words, while others might be working on digraphs or other skills, depending on students' needs. Students should read appropriate decodable texts to practice those skills.
- Some groups may read the decodable texts quickly and accurately, and be ready to move on to less decodable texts. April says, "We're not going to belabor the process and make them read it again if they read it automatically on the first try. They've reached the goal!" Other groups may need more time reading decodable texts to get more practice.
- Students who are reading accurately and automatically should work on other areas of fluency, such as phrasing and expression.

The goal is to move students out of decodable texts and into authentic texts as soon as they are ready (ideally by second grade). Decodable texts are like training wheels on a bike. Kemeny says, at the beginning of second grade, she has her students read decodable books, but she transitions them into books that are less decodable, such as *Geodes*, before ultimately moving to authentic texts, as soon as they are ready (Episodes 92 and 134).

CHECK OUT OUR PODCAST, EPISODE 134

"Small-Group Instructional Time" with April Evans
Hear all about the texts, structure, and routines that April Evans uses in her first-grade classroom for small-group instruction. She tells how she uses decodable texts for students who need support with accuracy, automaticity, rate, and expression.

RELATED EPISODES
- **Episode 91:** "Improving Reading for Older Students, Part 2," with David Liben
- **Episode 92:** "Talking About the Literacy Block with Two Early Elementary Teachers" with April Evans and Danielle Hunter
- **Episode 98:** "Improving Student Reading Growth in Months with Fluency Instruction and Practice" with Lindsay Kemeny and Lorraine Griffith
- **Episode 164:** "Misconceptions About Learning to Read" with Carolyn Strom

I have a student who can sound out words but reads slowly. How do I provide support to increase automaticity?

ANSWER Jan Hasbrouck says that although some students master phonological awareness, decoding, and sight recognition of familiar words, they may still not read at a sufficient rate, and may benefit from fluency intervention. However, Jan cautioned, "We don't want to help them read fast... we want them to read well." So even though we want to improve reading rate, we do not want to overemphasize speed (Episode 153).

That means doing two things:

1. Continue to develop students' word recognition skills to become fluent, especially with multisyllabic or unfamiliar words.

2. Be sure students are still making meaning from what they are reading. Don't ignore phrasing and expression—an indicator of meaning making—while working to improve rate.

Also, keep in mind, nearly all students will need fluency instruction and practice after they have become accurate word readers. Tim Rasinski says that many educators believe that fluency is not important after the early grades because more of the classroom reading happens silently. But the way we read orally and the way we read silently are connected, so fluency instruction is necessary in upper elementary grades and can be helpful in middle school (Episode 62).

> "Fluency doesn't just go away. It's something that goes well beyond the primary grades."
>
> —**TIM RASINSKI, EPISODE 62**

As students age, the texts they are given become more challenging. They will encounter more difficult and less familiar vocabulary. The structure of sentences and paragraphs becomes more complex. So students need to continue working on fluency to comprehend those texts.

WHAT YOU CAN DO UnboundEd's Alice Wiggins, Brandon White, and colleagues (2020) say that "a cycle of repeated reading is a key scaffold that supports all students in reading grade-level text." Start by working with the student at the word level. Have him repeatedly read a list of words (e.g., *rainforest, tropical, canopy, temperate, habitat*), working to increase his rate with each reading.

Also, be mindful of comprehension, even at the word level. For example, if the student reads the word *tropical*, follow up with a question such as, "Can you think of a place that is *tropical*? What is it like?" You might even show a picture of a tropical location if he is unfamiliar with the word's meaning.

From there, work with the student on rate at the phrase level, starting with a list of phrases from a text you use in Tier 1 instruction. Give him a list of phrases, preferably ones that connect with content from ELA, science, or social studies. Have him read the phrases repeatedly until he reads them automatically, without sounding out words. Here is an example of a phrase list:

- rainforests are warm
- wet habitats
- canopy of the tropical rainforest
- temperate rainforests are cooler

Once the student is ready, let him practice the full passage, weaving in work on expression. Here is an example of a passage:

> Rainforests are warm, wet habitats. Trees in the rainforest grow very tall. They must compete with other plants for sunlight. The canopy of the tropical rainforest is over one hundred feet above ground. Temperate rainforests are cooler than tropical rainforests.

CHECK OUT OUR PODCAST, EPISODE 79

"What Does Equitable ELA Instruction Require?"
with Brandon White and Alice Wiggins In this episode, we talked with UnboundED's Brandon White and Alice Wiggins about effective and equitable ELA instruction, including the benefits of fluency instruction that supports all students.

RELATED EPISODES

- **Episode 62:** "Effective Fluency Instruction" with Tim Rasinski
- **Episodes 90 and 91:** "Improving Reading for Older Students, Parts 1 and 2," with David Liben
- **Episode 153:** "Science of Reading Beyond Phonics: Fluency Instruction and Assessment" with Jan Hasbrouck

TEACHING TOOL

Syllable Pyramids

Syllable Pyramids are a tool for working on rate at the word level. With them, students read one syllable at a time of a multisyllabic word in the pyramid. Then they reread the syllables until they can read the full word smoothly and fluently. Quickly and gently correct mispronunciations, and always help students understand the meaning of the word to help them orthographically map it.

Syllable Pyramid
Three- Syllable Words

rain
rain-for
rain-for-est
rainforest

can
can-o
can-o-py
canopy

trop
trop-i
trop-i-cal
tropical

temp
temp-er
temp-er-ate
temperate

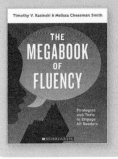

A Helpful Resource for Planning for Fluency Instruction
Tim Rasinski and Melissa Cheesman Smith's *The Megabook of Fluency* contains many examples of syllable pyramids, along with other strategies to engage students and boost their reading skills.

I've heard that one-minute oral reading fluency assessments are important. What can I learn from them?

ANSWER Jan Hasbrouck told us that the last 40 years of research on fluency assessment show that measuring the number of words students read correctly per minute is one of the best indicators of comprehension. But she was also clear that those assessments do not fully measure fluency or, by extension, comprehension. She compared a teacher administering an oral reading fluency assessment to a doctor taking your temperature. Your temperature can't tell a doctor everything that's right or wrong with you, but it's a quick way to know if your health is off track and figure out next steps to take (Episode 153). (Learn more about the connection between reading fluency and comprehension in Question 3.2.)

Jan and her former professor, Gerald Tindal, collected data on hundreds of thousands of students to determine oral reading fluency norms, which is captured in their oral reading fluency charts below.

Oral Reading Fluency (ORF) Data

Grade	Percentile	Fall WCPM*	Winter WCPM*	Spring WCPM*
1	90		97	116
	75		59	91
	50		29	60
	25		16	34
	10		9	18
2	90	111	131	148
	75	84	109	124
	50	50	84	100
	25	36	59	72
	10	23	35	43
3	90	134	161	166
	75	104	137	139
	50	83	97	112
	25	59	79	91
	10	40	62	63

Grade	Percentile	Fall WCPM*	Winter WCPM*	Spring WCPM*
4	90	153	168	184
	75	125	143	160
	50	94	120	133
	25	75	95	105
	10	60	71	83
5	90	179	183	195
	75	153	160	169
	50	121	133	146
	25	87	109	119
	10	64	84	102
6	90	185	195	204
	75	159	166	173
	50	132	145	146
	25	112	116	122
	10	89	91	91

*WCPM = Words Correct Per Minute

(Hasbrouck & Tindal, 2017)

> "[ORF] is like a thermometer. Thermometers don't diagnose broken legs or some other things, but they tell us a lot. ORF tells us a lot, and it does tell us quite a bit about comprehension."
>
> —JAN HASBROUCK, EPISODE 153

You may think that the higher the score, the better. Interestingly, though, average is *good*! Jan says that between 50 and 75 percent is optimal (Episode 153). There is no evidence that there is any value of students scoring above 75 percent. In fact, if students score above 75 percent, they may be reading so quickly that they are not comprehending very well. If students score below 50 percent, consider looking more closely at what they need to improve. According to Hasbrouck and Tindal, they may need a fluency-building program (2017).

WHAT YOU CAN DO The ORF assessment is informal and quick. To administer it, you:

- give the student a copy of a grade-level passage.
- time him for one minute as he reads it aloud.
- mark errors on your copy of the passage.
- count the number of words the student read correctly.
- identify where the student's WCPM (words correct per minute) falls on the norms chart.

Here are some quick tips from Jan Hasbrouck on administering the ORF.

Stopwatch Etiquette

Instead of saying "Ready, set, go" and starting the timer, tell the student to start whenever she is ready: "When you're ready, start reading," and then start your timer.

Marking Errors

The biggest question on scoring an ORF assessment is probably, "What counts as an error?" Here are some answers:

- If a student pronounces a word incorrectly multiple times, count each time as an error.
- If a student transposes two words (e.g., the text says, "black cat," but the student reads "cat black"), count that as two errors.
- If a student omits a word, count each omitted word as an error.
- If a student inserts a word, don't count it as an error because that word is not on the page.

Speed Readers

Don't encourage or allow the student to speed read. If she starts reading too quickly, she is most likely trying to impress you. Say: "Wow! You can read really fast!" and have her reread the text like she's talking to someone (Episode 153).

CHECK OUT OUR PODCAST, EPISODE 153

"Science of Reading Beyond Phonics: Fluency Instruction and Assessment" with Jan Hasbrouck

In this episode, you can hear Jan Hasbrouck talk in detail about oral reading fluency assessments, the Hasbrouck and Tindal oral reading fluency norms chart, and all things fluency.

RELATED EPISODE

- **Episode 110:** "Baltimore Secondary Literacy Teachers Talk Fluency" with Tanisha Dasmunshi, Emily Jaskowski, and Emery Uwimana

TEACHING TOOL

Fluency Tracker

Here's a tip from teachers in Baltimore, Maryland. Emily Jaskowski, an eighth-grade teacher, motivated her students by sharing their growth in words per minute over the year. And when seventh-grade teacher Emery Uwimana's seventh-grade students tracked their progress, they saw evidence of their growth. It was concrete, and they really responded to that. Emery says, "You see the improvement, and you see that THEY see the improvement within themselves. It's awesome. That's my favorite part. They hear themselves read from January, and then in March they're like, 'I'm so much better. I'm so dope'" (Episode 110).

Use a tracker like this one for students to track their WCPM scores after each ORF assessment and see their growth over the course of the year.

FLUENCY TRACKER
Keep track of the number of words you can read correctly in just one minute!

Words Correct Per Minute	FALL			WINTER			SPRING		
190									
180									
170									
160									
150									
140									
130									
120									
110									
100									
90									
80									
70									
60									
50									

FOURTH GRADE Words Correct Per Minute Goals		
Fall	Winter	Spring
94–125	120–143	133–160

Download the "Fluency Tracker."

The oral reading fluency assessment does not measure expression. So what can I use to measure it?

ANSWER The oral reading fluency (ORF) assessment measures only accuracy and rate. Although it is possible to listen for expression during an ORF assessment, it's better to listen to a student read longer than one minute to get a more accurate picture. So how do you measure expression?

Tim Rasinski's Multidimensional Fluency Rubric allows you to measure not only expression, but also volume, phrasing, smoothness, and pace. Unlike the ORF assessment, which has a specific formula to follow, as students read orally you will need to decide where they fall on the scale—for instance, you will have to make a judgment whether students are reading smoothly with some breaks, reading with occasional breaks in rhythm, reading with extended pauses or hesitations, or frequently hesitating. There is more teacher judgment involved with this assessment than there is with the ORF, but it can help you get a picture of where students are with expression and how you can help them improve.

A score of 10 or more indicates students are making good progress in fluency, and a score below 10 indicates they need additional fluency instruction (Rasinski, 2004).

MULTIDIMENSIONAL FLUENCY RUBRIC

	1	2	3	4
Expression and Volume	Reads in a quiet voice as if to get words out. The reading does not sound natural like talking to a friend.	Reads in a quiet voice. The reading sounds natural in part of the text, but the reader does not always sound like they are talking to a friend.	Reads with volume and expression. However, sometimes the reader slips into expressionless reading and does not sound like they are talking to a friend.	Reads with varied volume and expression. The reader sounds like they are talking to a friend with their voice matching the interpretation of the passage.
Phrasing	Reads word-by-word in a monotone voice.	Reads in two or three word phrases, not adhering to punctuation, stress, and intonation.	Reads with a mixture of run-ons, mid-sentence pauses for breath, and some choppiness. There is reasonable stress and intonation.	Reads with good phrasing, adhering to punctuation, stress, and intonation.
Smoothness	Frequently hesitates while reading, sounds out words, and repeats words or phrases. The reader makes multiple attempts to read the same passage.	Reads with extended pauses or hesitations. The reader has many "rough spots."	Reads with occasional breaks in rhythm. The reader has difficulty with specific words and/or sentence structures.	Reads smoothly with some breaks, but self-corrects with difficult words and/or sentence structures.
Pace	Reads slowly and laboriously.	Reads moderately slowly.	Reads generally at an appropriate rate throughout reading.	Reads at an appropriate conversational pace throughout the reading.

(Zutell and Rasinski, 1991)

Download the "Multidimensional Fluency Rubric."

WHAT YOU CAN DO If the last thing you want to do is give your students another assessment, you're in luck because you can assess expression informally. Anytime students read aloud, pay attention to the areas on the Multidimensional Fluency Rubric and take notes as you listen. You can also have students record themselves reading aloud if that helps you to assess. And of course, the obvious follow-up question: What do you do if students are not reading with expression? Here are a couple ideas:

Explain Why Expression Matters

Expression matters because our brains are wired to understand speech. So If we make reading sound like speech, it will be easier for our brains to comprehend the text. Jan Hasbrouck suggests explaining this to students, so they see why it matters (Episode 153).

Try Echo Reading

Echo reading is particularly helpful for improving the components on the Multidimensional Fluency Rubric. Here are some tips to make it successful.

- Choose a short passage that you and students read in its entirety.
- If you are working with a text over multiple days, gradually increase the length of the text that you read and students echo. For instance, after a day or two, perhaps you can read two sentences before they echo.
- Have students read the text as they echo. No memorizing!
- Be dramatic! Make sure students see where you are pausing and how you change your voice to match the text.
- If you see students who are not reading with expression, pause and have them practice again.

 CHECK OUT OUR PODCAST, EPISODE 108

"From 13% to 100% Literacy Proficiency" with Angie Hanlin Listen to Angie Hanlin, a school leader from Wisconsin, talk about the importance of improving fluency and the power of setting individual fluency goals.

RELATED EPISODE

- **Episode 153:** "Science of Reading Beyond Phonics: Fluency Instruction and Assessment" with Jan Hasbrouck

What kinds of texts should I use for fluency instruction and practice?

ANSWER There are three major considerations when choosing texts for fluency instruction and practice: length, content, and difficulty.

Text Length

Generally speaking, fluency passages should be about 50 to 200 words. They should be on the shorter side so students can read them repeatedly without it feeling laborious. That means for beginning readers, stay on the low end of that range, and as students build their fluency, move up the range (Honig, Diamond, & Gutlohn, 2018). Don't stress about counting every last word!

Text Content

Brandon White advises us to use "grade-level texts that are rigorous with rich vocabulary, and have students practice repeatedly reading those texts" (Episode 79). Fluency practice will help students understand the text more deeply, which will build their capability and confidence in Tier 1 instruction. It will help them answer difficult questions about the text, as well as have conversations and write about it. It will also feel more purposeful for the students because they will see connections between fluency, vocabulary, and knowledge.

> "The passage they read was a speech in *Animal Farm*. We practiced it a bunch of times, and then a ton of kids were excited to perform it for everybody else."
>
> —TANISHA DASMUNSHI, EPISODE 110

Text Difficulty

Don't be afraid to use challenging texts. There is a growing body of evidence that supports more challenging texts for reading instruction and practice in general, and for fluency instruction and practice in particular. In a study focused on repeated readings, Steven Stahl and Kathleen Heubach (2005) found that students made the most progress when texts were at their frustration level. That may sound counterintuitive, but the researchers discovered that with quality instruction, practice, and support, students were able to accelerate their progress in reading by repeatedly reading those texts. Remember, these are short passages, not the entire text (Episode 62). (Read more about text levels in Question 5.7.)

WHAT YOU CAN DO We talked to three middle school teachers who told us their initial instinct was to give easier texts to students who were reading below grade level. But they used texts from their grade-level curriculum—and it was a wise decision. The teachers told us that the students improved their fluency when reading those texts for fluency practice. But maybe even more importantly, the teachers noticed that they showed more confidence in class discussions. They would be the first students to raise their hands to answer a question because they now understood the text more deeply from the fluency practice (Episode 110).

Texts for Fluency Practice

When choosing a text from your grade-level, Tier 1 curriculum, think about a short, high-impact passage that is worth reading multiple times. It could be a paragraph from a text that students need to reread to understand it fully, such as a paragraph from *Amos & Boris* that contains the words *phosphorescent* and *luminous*. Or it might be a pivotal paragraph from a novel that you don't want students to miss, such as an important speech from *Animal Farm*.

In some cases, it may not make sense to choose a text from your Tier 1 curriculum. You may want to consider other texts that connect to the topic students are studying in ELA, social studies, or science. For instance, when Lindsay Kemeny's class was learning about the rainforest, she would choose a variety of passages on that topic for fluency practice. That way, her students were seeing similar vocabulary and building their world knowledge, as they were developing fluency by reading the passages.

 CHECK OUT OUR PODCAST, EPISODE 110

"Baltimore Secondary Literacy Teachers Talk Fluency" with Tanisha Dasmunshi, Emily Jaskowski, and Emery Uwimana In this episode, three teachers talk about fluency assessment and instruction, and the impact it made on their middle-school students. The teachers give concrete tips for how they improved their students' fluency within the ELA class.

RELATED EPISODES

- **Episode 62:** "Effective Fluency Instruction" with Tim Rasinski
- **Episode 79:** "What Does Equitable ELA Instruction Require?" with Brandon White and Alice Wiggins

CHAPTER 4

VOCABULARY

Vocabulary instruction builds understanding of word meanings, parts, and histories, and greatly influences comprehension.

LORI'S STORY

I have so many joyful memories of teaching vocabulary—and stressful ones! One year, when I was teaching fifth grade, my students were reading *Shipwreck at the Bottom of the World*, a book about Ernest Shackleton's 1914 Antarctic voyage. We trekked through the book's rich vocabulary, using Frayer models, acting out words, and working in groups to figure out words in context.

Because kids—and we adults, too—are always learning and practicing vocabulary, I worked hard to teach vocabulary words. But that was messy. It meant I had to determine which words to teach, and when and how to teach them. My students were memorizing words without retaining their meanings. A co-teacher asked me, "Are you trying to teach individual words or explore words and word parts?" That question got me thinking. I shifted gears. Instead of teaching isolated words, we began to find connected words and pull them apart—asking questions about the parts and where the word came from. I noticed students' approaching vocabulary words with piqued interest and curiosity. Even more, they retained meanings and used the words in speaking and writing.

Questions That Keep You Up at Night

4.1   What's the connection between vocabulary and comprehension?

4.2   I can't possibly teach students every word in the English language! What are ways students learn words without being taught them directly?

4.3   How do I promote curiosity about learning words that I don't teach directly?

4.4   What is the role of oral language in developing vocabulary?

4.5   What are morphology and etymology—and what do they have to do with vocabulary?

4.6   How does content-rich ELA instruction improve vocabulary?

4.7   What are Tier 1, Tier 2, and Tier 3 words?

4.8   How do I choose words to teach?

4.9   How do I teach vocabulary? What are some research-based methods?

4.10   What strategies are helpful for teaching vocabulary?

What's the connection between vocabulary and comprehension?

ANSWER Vocabulary plays an important role in determining whether we understand what we read and has a strong effect on comprehension (McKeown, Beck, Omanson, & Perfetti, 1983). In fact, the National Reading Panel (NRP) placed vocabulary within its report's comprehension chapter, citing a causal relationship between vocabulary and comprehension. In order to comprehend, we need to understand and process words. So it's nearly impossible to separate vocabulary from comprehension.

Author and professor Doug Fisher asserts, "We don't learn words in isolation. We learn concepts, and vocabulary are the labels for those concepts." He gave us an example using the word *train*. We need to have a concept of *train* in order to label the word. If we have never seen or learned about a train, we don't know what it looks like or how it sounds or what its purpose is, so we won't be able to add that word to our vocabulary. Or we might confuse the noun *train* with the verb *train*—as in, "train your dog." However, if we have the knowledge about both forms of the word, we can label *train* accordingly (Episode 158).

> "Vocabulary is a significant predictor to whether or not you understand what you read."
>
> —DOUG FISHER, EPISODE 158

So what does that mean for vocabulary's role in reading comprehension? One word: knowledge. We need knowledge to make sense of concepts we encounter in texts. We may access prior knowledge and combine it with new knowledge, or build new knowledge altogether. Knowledge is critical to comprehending, and vocabulary is knowledge of words and their meanings. Nancy Hennessy, author of *The Reading Comprehension Blueprint*, thinks about vocabulary as "active processing of the word" as well as the ability to transfer and connect understandings to various contexts (Episode 157). (For more information on the importance of background knowledge, check out Question 5.3.)

WHAT YOU CAN DO Doug Fisher reminds us that when we encounter a word with multiple meanings while we're reading, we activate all known definitions of that word and then use that knowledge to determine the meaning (Episode 158). Let's say students encounter the word *dusting* while reading. What might come to mind? Maybe dusting, as in dusting the coffee table? Or maybe dusting, as in a dusting of snow on the ground? Or maybe dusting, as in crop dusting a corn field? If students only know one meaning of *dusting*, that word isn't going to make sense to them in more than one context. That's why we need to help them develop a depth of understanding about words, which requires building knowledge and vocabulary simultaneously. Here are three effective ways to do that:

1. Read aloud and/or have students read knowledge-building, grade-level texts. (For more on read-alouds, see Question 5.8).

2. Select and create text sets to build knowledge and vocabulary—texts grouped around a specific topic, such as outer space, the five senses, or the Great Depression.

3. Promote wide reading of texts on specific topics. You might do that for early-elementary students by offering table baskets and take-home books, and for upper-elementary students by offering multimedia resources (Achieve the Core). Use the log on the next page to help students track their reading.

Moreover, pre-teaching vocabulary helps students acquire and remember information in texts (Medo & Ryder, 1993). And regularly providing students with opportunities to connect speaking and writing to text allows for increased repetition and practice.

 CHECK OUT OUR PODCAST, EPISODE 158

"Science of Reading Beyond Phonics: The Ultimate Goal of Reading" with Doug Fisher In this episode, Doug Fisher amplifies the connectedness of vocabulary and comprehension, underscoring the pivotal role of knowledge.

RELATED EPISODE

- **Episode 157:** "Science of Reading Beyond Phonics: Reading Comprehension Blueprint" with Nancy Hennessy

Knowledge and Vocabulary Log

This log gives students a space to capture the knowledge and vocabulary they've learned from texts and text sets.

1. Have students read, watch, or listen to each text.

2. Ask them to consider: "What did you learn about this topic?" "How did this text help to build your knowledge and vocabulary?"

3. Have them continue this process for each text on the topic.

KNOWLEDGE AND VOCABULARY LOG

Topic	Text	What did you learn? (knowledge + vocabulary)	How did this text build your knowledge and vocabulary?	Write a six-word summary.
		Write, draw and label, or list.		
Outer Space	*Moonshot* by Brian Floca (book)	• Events of the Apollo 11 mission • Astronauts walked on the moon July 20, 1969.	I knew that people walked on the moon, but I didn't know who did it first! Astronauts Neil Armstrong and Buzz Aldrin walked on the moon. Michael Collins continued to orbit the moon.	Daring mission to explore the moon.
Outer Space	"Kids Britannica Homework Help: Moon" (article)	• The moon orbits the Earth. The moon also spins. • Earth is affected by the moon's gravity. • The moon doesn't change shape.	Learned more about the moon's shape and surface to better visualize the Apollo 11 mission and landing on the moon.	Moon orbits Earth; doesn't change shape.
Outer Space	*Counting on Katherine: How Katherine Johnson Saved Apollo 13* by Helaine Becker (book)	• NASA—National Aeronautics and Space Administration • Rocket ships launch like throwing a ball into the air (a curved path). • The Moon's gravity can act like a slingshot.	How do spaceships get to the moon? People like Katherine Johnson made sure flight paths were safe and accurate.	Spaceships launch; curved paths and gravity.

Download the "Knowledge and Vocabulary Log."

(Adapted from Achieve the Core Rolling Knowledge and Vocabulary Template)

I can't possibly teach students every word in the English language! What are ways students learn words without being taught them directly?

ANSWER Students need to learn approximately 2,000 to 3,000 words per year (PaTTAN, 2019). If you're doing the math like we are, you realize it's impossible to teach every word explicitly. And while our students learn many, many words from spoken language and the world around them, richer vocabulary comes from texts (Episode 158). So yes, we do have to teach some words explicitly—with direct instruction that includes definitions, examples, and practice opportunities. But vocabulary is an unconstrained skill, which researcher and professor Kristin Conradi Smith defines as a meaning-based skill that grows across a lifetime. So we must continue to learn new words and about words limitlessly (Episode 143).

What are ways students learn words? Students learn words through rich texts, discussions, writing, and teacher modeling of academic vocabulary. As they learn concepts, vocabulary provides labels to help them make sense of and connect those concepts. When we intentionally integrate word learning into daily learning experiences, we support students in acquiring vocabulary that sticks.

The vocabulary and syntax of written language differs from oral language, so it's important to teach students vocabulary routines for both that they can apply independently. By teaching word-learning strategies, you help students access the meaning of unfamiliar words, without direct instruction. It strengthens decoding and fluency instruction, too. (Learn more about the role of oral language in developing vocabulary in Question 4.4.)

WHAT YOU CAN DO Professor Emeritus Claude Goldenberg explains that to orthographically map words, we connect sounds to spellings to meanings. Skillful readers do that quickly and automatically (Episodes 152 and 164). Here are some ways to connect sounds to letters to meanings in order to build automaticity.

> "Decoding isn't just mapping, like blending sounds together. It is attaching meaning. So there's a very important place for vocabulary development and word knowledge within decoding instruction."
>
> —CAROLYN STROM, EPISODE 164

Read aloud and/or have students read complex texts.

Complex texts can be grouped together by topic to build knowledge and vocabulary. Doing so supports students in learning related words about a topic as they also build knowledge on that topic. Read-alouds are one way that students can access complex texts to build knowledge, vocabulary, and syntax. (For more information on read-alouds, head to Question 5.8.)

Investigate word parts and origins.

Investigating word parts and origins should start early. Morphology and etymology can help you do that. Once students know a word's parts, or morphemes, they can create definitions, locate synonyms and antonyms, and determine shades of meaning. Learning a word's history, or etymology, helps them arrive at meanings, connect words with similar parts, and identify spelling patterns.

Encourage students to use new vocabulary in speaking and writing.

If you don't use it, you lose it. Repetition is key for retention, so get students using the vocabulary words they learn. Can they "catch" one another using words? Might they create a vocabulary wall that they add to as they learn about topics? Could you give them sticky notes with words written on them and challenge them to use the words throughout the day? Or maybe they play word-association games to solidify vocabulary and content knowledge? This is where the art—and fun—of teaching shines through!

By providing students with opportunities for speaking and writing using vocabulary, along with teaching them routines for independent application, you increase word learning and comprehension, without directly instructing.

CHECK OUT OUR PODCAST, EPISODE 152

**"Science of Reading For ALL Students: Multilingual Learners"
with Claude Goldenberg** In this episode, Claude Goldenberg explores the process of orthographically mapping words by connecting phonemes to graphemes to semantics. And he debunks a myth that the science of reading applies only to monolingual English speakers.

RELATED EPISODES

- **Episode 143:** "Maximizing Small-Group Reading Instruction" with Kristin Conradi Smith, Steven Amendum, and Tamara Williams
- **Episode 158:** "Science of Reading Beyond Phonics: The Ultimate Goal of Reading" with Doug Fisher
- **Episode 164:** "Misconceptions About Learning to Read" with Carolyn Strom

How do I promote curiosity about learning words that I don't teach directly?

ANSWER Our goal is for our students to become lifelong readers and writers, which means giving them the tools to understand words instead of teaching them every word. Since we only have 180-ish days with our students each school year, balancing teaching words explicitly and promoting ways to understand words independently is super important.

To promote curiosity about words, help students understand what words are and how they are built. Remember, almost all words are bases—like LEGO® bases! They have structures: large parts, small parts, and in-between parts. When students play with words—take them apart, mix them around, put them together—they come to understand how word parts work together and what words mean, and that builds a deeper understanding of vocabulary specifically and language generally. So it's important to teach students ways to manipulate words to make meaning and construct semantic networks—knowledge-building "maps" in the mind that connect related concepts and information. This is far more effective than teaching vocabulary and concepts in silos, with no connection to each other (Episode 155). (For more information on giving students tools to understand words, see Question 4.2.)

WHAT YOU CAN DO For students to become proficient readers and writers, they need to read and/or listen to rich, complex texts—and discuss the words they contain. According to researchers Anne Cunningham and Keith Stanovich, "Books have 50% more rare words in them than adult prime-time television..." (2001). Author Robert Pondiscio reminds us that sophisticated language is more present in texts than in adult conversations (Episode 146). To grow vocabulary, students need to be exposed to words that are not in their vocabulary. Reading texts on topics students are studying ensures exposure and makes words stick.

Providing students access to rich, complex texts at grade level is necessary to increase students' interactions with words, build curiosity about vocabulary, and spur learning of Tier 2 and Tier 3 words. (See Question 4.7 for definitions of tiers of words.) In primary grades, that occurs mostly during read-alouds. In

> "Every single word is or contains a base. That's the part that carries the majority of the meaning. If you start there, it helps to build mental models of the entire system."
>
> **—LYN STONE, EPISODE 155**

intermediate and middle grades, it occurs mostly in ELA and the content areas, during in-class reading and teacher read-alouds (Ness, 2024). Rich, complex texts provide the opportunity for students to use context clues to determine word meanings.

Kory Jensen, a fourth-grade teacher from Aurora, Colorado, explains how he promotes curiosity about words in his classroom. When he teaches a morpheme such as the prefix *in-*, he tells students its meaning: *not*, *in*, or *into*. From there, students create morpheme cards that allow them to manipulate word parts to build whole words. Kory says, "It's not about teaching every word. It is about teaching the word parts and their meanings." This builds confidence and curiosity for learning about words.

Here are three practical and easy ideas for promoting curiosity about words.

1. Integrate Tier 2 and Tier 3 vocabulary within decoding and fluency instruction. This practice provides students with repeated exposures to store the word in long-term memory.

2. Use oral language—everyday and academic talk—to provide opportunities for students to hear and use Tier 2 and Tier 3 vocabulary. We can model using Tier 2 words in everyday vocabulary. Instead of saying we feel *happy*, we might use words like *gleeful* or *content*. Instead of *walking* to our bathroom break, we might *saunter* or *strut*.

3. Establish repeatable strategies, such as those we suggest in Question 4.10, to help students access vocabulary when reading independently.

CHECK OUT OUR PODCAST, EPISODE 146

"Reading Comprehension Is Not a Skill" with Robert Pondiscio In this episode, Robert Pondiscio discusses the robust knowledge and vocabulary base of good readers and asserts that students need to read more to gain rich vocabulary due to the complexities of text.

RELATED EPISODE

- **Episode 155:** "Science of Reading Beyond Phonics: Language for Life" with Lyn Stone

What is the role of oral language in developing vocabulary?

ANSWER When young children have strong oral language skills, they have a better chance at reading and writing success. And, unfortunately, the opposite is true: When they have weak oral language skills, they tend to struggle later in school (National Institute of Child Health and Human Development, 2010). Dr. Errick L. Greene, superintendent of Jackson Public Schools, says that because some students come to school with thousands more words in their oral vocabulary, we have to accelerate vocabulary development for other students through oral language (Episode 47).

Oral language includes receptive language (listening) and expressive language (speaking). Students naturally learn everyday receptive and expressive language, but not necessarily academic language. Books and other types of instructional materials contain words that we don't use every day. The syntax, or structure of a sentence, of academic language is more complex than everyday language, too. Furthermore, the academic language that students engage in as they interact with texts before, during, and after reading positively impacts oral language skills, which include vocabulary learning (Episode 116).

Young children come to us with stronger listening comprehension skills than reading comprehension skills. Why? Because they haven't yet developed the ability to decode rich texts. That's why reading aloud rich, complex texts is so important, and not just in early grades. Students in all grades benefit from the powerful oral-language experiences that read-alouds of rich, complex text ensure. Read-alouds enhance language skills and build content knowledge (Ness, 2024). When we read aloud to students and discuss texts, students actively listen and ask questions. They are developing verbal reasoning skills, such as making inferences and understanding of figurative language and speech. To do that, they activate prior knowledge and build new knowledge to connect with and make sense of the text.

Read-alouds bridge the gap between listening comprehension and reading comprehension. The younger the students are, the wider the gap between those two forms of comprehension. As students grow, the gap decreases and levels out at about eighth grade (Episode 158).

It's our job as teachers to help students develop strong oral language skills. But how? (For more on interactive read-alouds, head to Question 5.8.)

> "Language supports literacy, but also literacy supports language."
>
> **—ELSA CÁRDENAS-HAGAN, EPISODE 119**

WHAT YOU CAN DO There are three steps you can take to strengthen students' oral language skills, positively affecting vocabulary. This process helps students learn habits to process complex text, such as pausing to think and ask questions then conversing to make sense of learning.

Here's a three-step process inspired by our conversation with Associate Professor, Florida State University, Sonia Cabell.

1. **Build content knowledge and vocabulary through read-alouds or reading complex texts.** Engage with multiple rich texts on the same topic and guide students through text with pre-planned stopping points.

2. **Ask open-ended questions.** Listen to what students say and build on their ideas by adding information, probing further, or asking follow-up questions. This is an opportunity to model academic talk through phrases such as "Say more about that..." or "How did you choose to...?" (Episode 116).

3. **Facilitate content-rich conversations.** Have students practice using vocabulary words in oral language experiences connected to text.

A Helpful Resource for Developing Oral Language and Vocabulary In *Strive-for-Five Conversations,* Tricia Zucker and Sonia Cabell share an easy-to-implement framework to engage children in responsive conversations that go beyond the surface for deeper understanding.

 CHECK OUT OUR PODCAST, EPISODE 116

"Sonia Cabell on the Importance of Content-Rich ELA Instruction" In this episode, Sonia Cabell shares the importance of oral language and content-rich ELA instruction for reading development. The benefits go beyond reading to writing, with oral language as the bridge.

RELATED EPISODES

- **Episode 47:** "Jackson's Journey to HQIM" with Errick L. Greene
- **Episode 139:** "Knowledge and Comprehension" with Daniel Willingham and Barbara Davidson
- **Episode 158:** "Science of Reading Beyond Phonics: The Ultimate Goal of Reading" with Doug Fisher

Routine for a Multi-Component Approach

Including vocabulary in decoding and fluency instruction is critical for all learners, especially multilingual learners. Developmental psychologist Melissa Orkin and colleagues call that a multi-component approach and recommend discussing the meanings of words and word parts when teaching early-reading skills (2022). Starting this process early helps children thread sound to symbol to meaning, and it should continue into the upper-elementary and middle grades.

A MULTI-COMPONENT APPROACH TO DECODING, FLUENCY, AND VOCABULARY INSTRUCTION

Word	What's the word?	*bug*
Say It	Say it out loud— many times—and have students repeat.	/b/ /u/ /g/ = *bug* Turn to a partner and say the word *bug*. Whisper the word *bug* into your whisper phone. Jump up and down three times and say *bug* every time your feet touch the ground.
Sound It	Count the sounds, or phonemes, in the word.	There are three sounds in the word *bug*.
Connect It	Read and spell the word and similar words.	*bug* = b, u, g B – *bop, big, burp* Ug – *tug, mug, hug, shrug*
Define It	Define the word and share the part of speech. Learn the morphology and etymology.	The CVC word *bug* is a noun and a verb with many meanings. Let's focus on several meanings of *bug*. **bug** (noun): an insect **bug** (noun): a sickness **bug** (verb): to bother, annoy How does the history of the word *bug* connect with the word's meanings? *Bug* may come from Middle English *bugge*, which means something frightening. It's likely connected to the Scottish word *bogill*, which means goblin or bugbear.
Contextualize It	Provide examples of how it's used in sentences.	There is a bug on the leaf. My brother has a stomach bug and was sick all night. Can you bug your mom again about having a sleepover tonight?
Play With It	Add prefixes, suffixes, etc.	How does adding the suffix *–ed* change the word *bug*? What about *–ing*? **bugged** (the g doubles, past tense) **bugging** (the g doubles, present tense, active verb) What happens if we add the prefix *de–*? **debug** (meaning changes: prefix *de–* means away, away from, out of) Are there any words we can put together with bug? Jitter + bug Litter + bug Lady + bug Love + bug

Download the "Multi-Component Approach to Decoding, Fluency, and Vocabulary Instruction" planner.

What are morphology and etymology—and what do they have to do with vocabulary?

ANSWER Morphology and etymology are "units of language that work together" (Episode 155). They go together like peanut butter and jelly (unless you have students with a peanut allergy!). They're a perfect pair. They help us understand words better because they require us to learn all about what makes words words.

Morphology

According to literacy expert Barbara Foorman and colleagues, morphology is knowledge of meaningful word parts in a language—typically prefixes, suffixes, roots, and base words (2016). Morphemes are the smallest grammatical unit of speech. Elsa Cárdenas-Hagan, author of *Teaching English Language Learners: The Foundations of Literacy*, says that within words, there are small meaning units that can be beneficial for expanding your vocabulary (Episode 119). Sometimes morphemes can stand on their own, such as *tool*, and sometimes they need to connect with other morphemes to form a word, such as *re-*. When we combine morphemes, we create whole new words—for example, *re + tool = retool* (Shanahan, 2018). By the age of 10, morphological awareness is a better predictor of decoding ability than phonological awareness (Mann & Singson, 2003). If that's not motivation to teach morphemes, we don't know what is!

Etymology

Etymology is the study of word origins—where words come from and how they've found their way into how language is used today. It explains why the morphemes are the way they are and lets us know how to pronounce and even spell words.

It might seem like a great idea to teach from a list of morphemes with etymology information for each one. You can find such a list in linguist Lyn Stone's book *Language for Life*, but Lyn herself claims, "the best word list is a book" (Episode 155). She cautions against teaching from a list because students need to be able to connect and label words based on their meaning. To do so, they need to activate prior knowledge and build schema, and the best way to do that is by reading. See the connection between knowledge and vocabulary here, too? They're inextricable! (To learn about schemas and how to activate prior knowledge, check out Question 5.4.)

WHAT YOU CAN DO Integrate morphology and etymology into daily instruction to help students become, as Lyn Stone says, "wordsmiths." The capacity to play with and study words has no limits.

In the primary grades, integrating morphology might mean adding word play to your phonics instruction. Your students can pull words apart and move around their letters and sounds to create new words, think more deeply about words, letters, and sounds, and discuss their meanings. In the upper-elementary and middle grades, it might mean choosing vocabulary words to explore from a text students are reading or will read, particularly high-utility Tier 2 or Tier 3 words. (See Question 4.7 for definitions of tiers of words.)

Regardless of grade level, integrating etymology entails teaching where words come from. Understanding etymology gets students curious about words and their origins and helps with spelling, too. Your students can add this information to a vocabulary wall or journal for reference when reading, speaking, or writing. Understanding and manipulating words and word parts will help students become better readers, speakers, and writers.

Furthermore, Elsa Cárdenas-Hagan says that cognates can help multilingual learners develop their vocabulary. A cognate is a word in one language, such as *family* in English, that is similar in spelling and meaning to a word in another language, such as *familia* in Spanish. Just over one-third of English words are cognates, which can help to bridge the gap to learning English (Episode 119).

A Helpful Resource for Teaching Multisyllabic and Multimorphemic Words
Words are so much fun to play with, especially for elementary students! Reading multisyllabic and multimorphemic words, and learning how words work, enhances reading proficiency. To learn more, pick up Heidi Anne Mesmer's *Big Words for Young Readers: Teaching Kids in Grades K to 5 to Decode—and Understand—Words With Multiple Syllables and Morphemes.*

CHECK OUT OUR PODCAST, EPISODE 155

"Science of Reading Beyond Phonics: Language for Life" with Lyn Stone In this episode, Lyn Stone talks all about the joy of playing with words—including the intersection of vocabulary with morphology and etymology—and the powerful impact of language and vocabulary on literacy development.

RELATED EPISODE

- **Episode 119:** "How Reading Science Works for English Learners" with Elsa Cárdenas-Hagan

TEACHING TOOL

Wordplay Framework

Use this Wordplay Framework when teaching decoding, practicing fluency, or reading a text. The goal is to connect the target word to its morphology and etymology, and consider related words to strengthen meaning. Teaching morphology and etymology creates pathways that help students better understand a target word and related words (Episode 155).

WORDPLAY FRAMEWORK

Instructional Function	Example	Morphology and Etymology	Brainstorm Related Words
Within Decoding	Teaching different sounds of the letter c, /k/ and /s/.	Introduce the morpheme *circ-* and provide a definition: *circ-* = circle or ring	*circle* *circular* *circus*
Within Fluency	Teaching the Preamble to the Constitution	Share the etymology of *constitution* from Latin: The word *constitute* means to make up, form, compose. *-tion* is a suffix meaning the act of or the result of.	*constitutional* *constitution* *constitute* *constitutes* *constituted*
Within a Text	Teaching the text *Good Masters! Sweet Ladies!*	Share the etymology of *medieval* from Latin *medium:* The root *-medi* means middle in Latin.	*immediate* *media* *medium* *multimedia* *mediator* *mediocre*

Download the "Wordplay Framework" planner.

How does content-rich ELA instruction improve vocabulary?

ANSWER Content-rich ELA instruction differs from content-area instruction because it focuses on ELA standards, using content knowledge and vocabulary to support learning. On the flip side, content-area instruction focuses on learning about topics, with content-area standards as the driver. Barbara Davidson, Executive Director of the Knowledge Matters Campaign and President of StandardsWork, shares five essential features of high-quality content-rich ELA instruction (Episode 139).

1. **Specific** Content-rich curriculum builds domain knowledge through topics, which is accomplished using a set of authentic grade-level texts on those topics, rather than "random acts of content" (Episode 139). Students gain knowledge and vocabulary by reading, speaking, and writing about a curated set of texts that dive deeply into a topic.

2. **Cumulative** It's important to think about students' experiences horizontally within their grade and vertically throughout their grades. The careful mapping of topics allows for sequential and scaffolded vocabulary and knowledge-building instruction, while steering clear of over-teaching and under-teaching topics.

3. **Inspiring and Well-Rounded** When students learn about topics related to science, history, or art and culture that interest them, they learn more. According to cognitive scientist Daniel Willingham, "The more you know, the more easily you learn new things. Knowledge improves your ability to remember new things, and it actually improves the quality and speed of your thinking" (2006). That facilitates a love of learning and builds curiosity about the world and words.

4. **Preparatory** The content should prepare students for future educational and life experiences. Whether they're learning about how the human body works, how to launch a spacecraft, or what life was like during the Revolutionary War, students learn important content and gain knowledge about words and the world.

> "I asked a student 'Why is it that you like writing so much more now than you did before?' and she said, 'Well, now I have something to write about.'"
>
> **—BARBARA DAVIDSON, EPISODE 139**

5. **Integrated and Rigorous** Students should be exposed to content and engage in tasks that meet grade-level ELA standards. They should read about what they write and write about what they read. They should never be at a loss for a topic to write about because, through instruction, they have deep content knowledge and vocabulary on many topics. Rigorous reading and writing experiences provide students opportunities to build, internalize, and convey content knowledge and vocabulary.

WHAT YOU CAN DO We all want a list or a schedule that is time-stamped for teaching vocabulary. But that's not quite the way it works. Our vocabularies are pliable... always changing and growing. Vocabulary is one of the most important markers for comprehension and there are dos and don'ts for instruction. Here are some helpful guidelines when thinking about vocabulary instruction (Episode 156):

DO...

- Integrate word learning within content-rich instruction.
- Explicitly teach vocabulary and word-learning strategies, including word consciousness (being aware of unknown words and applying strategies to figure them out).
- Encourage students to think about vocabulary while reading and listening, and using it when writing and speaking.
- Establish and maintain word-learning strategies, such as those we suggest in Question 4.10.

DON'T...

- Take a one-and-done approach to word learning.
- Teach words in isolation, give students lists of isolated words, or ask them to write words repeatedly.
- Engage students in word work that's disconnected from content.
- Try to teach students every word they will encounter. It's impossible and, research shows, ineffective.

Author and literacy expert Elsa Cárdenas-Hagan says, "Opportunities for vocabulary and comprehension really can occur across all the content areas. So we need to see ourselves as language, literacy, and content-area teachers" (Episode 119).

TEACHING TOOL

Vocabulary Flowchart

Follow this flowchart to build vocabulary and knowledge in your classroom. Where you start depends on whether you have a content-rich ELA curriculum.

If you do have content-rich ELA curriculum materials, such as those vetted by The Knowledge Matters Campaign advisory panel, you can enhance your instruction with these recommendations. If not, start at the beginning with topic selection. You can build knowledge and vocabulary sequentially and rigorously by thinking about topic, text, and words.

Topic Selection

- Choose science, history, or arts and culture topics as your guide to build knowledge during ELA.

Texts

- Build text sets around topics that include books, poems, music, podcasts, videos, and articles. (For example, if students are studying the human body and how food nourishes it, they might read books to increase their knowledge and vocabulary about the digestive system, read articles about various types of foods, watch a video of how food travels through the body, and so forth.)

Integrating Vocabulary

- Strategically plan for and explicitly teach vocabulary integrated across the day.
- Teach vocabulary-learning strategies, such as those we suggest in Question 4.10, and model how to use those strategies when encountering an unknown word in rich, complex texts.
- Build word-consciousness, which means being aware of unknown words and applying strategies to figure them out (Graves & Watts-Taffe, 2002).
- Use Tier 2 and Tier 3 words in classroom instruction and discourse (speaking and writing). (For definitions of tiers of words, see Question 4.7.)

What are Tier 1, Tier 2, and Tier 3 words?

ANSWER It's helpful to understand the categories and functions of words to teach vocabulary wisely. In 1985, vocabulary experts Isabel Beck and Margaret McKeown introduced the idea of dividing words into three tiers: Tier 1, Tier 2, and Tier 3 words.

Tier 1 words: high-frequency words used often in everyday language
Common words that students readily acquire through oral language experiences and do not necessarily require explicit instruction. Examples include *ball*, *see*, *run*, and *about*.

Tier 2 words: academic words used across domains such as science, social studies, and literature High-utility words that are often used in texts, but not in oral language. Examples include *contract*, *summon*, *feature*, *function*, and *abundant*.

Tier 3 words: content-specific words used, for the most part, within domains
Words that help us understand more deeply particular topics. Examples include *isotope*, *tundra*, *simile*, and *monarchy* (Episode 156).

> "Tier 2 words are words that are really, really important. They fall in science, social studies, and literature. They're used in multiple domains. They have high utility too."
>
> **—SEAN MORRISEY, EPISODE 156**

Tier 1 words are mostly acquired through oral language, as mentioned, but Tier 2 and Tier 3 are mostly acquired through explicit instruction and reading complex texts. Teaching those words improves students' understanding of word meanings and helps students comprehend text.

Students need to interact with a word around 12 times in order for it to "stick" (McKeown et al., 1983). That means students understand the word's meaning, the different ways it's used in oral and written language, and its relationship to other words. Our brains aren't organized like a dictionary. We learn "stuff" (including vocabulary) in related networks. For example, when you hear the word *water*, what concepts and other words pop into your mind? Maybe concepts such as the water cycle, oceans, or global warming, or words such as *marine*, *squid*, *luminous*, or *polluted*. When we connect concepts, we build semantic networks that help words and information stick. The more we can support students in reading, hearing, speaking, and writing Tier 2 and Tier 3 words, the higher probability that words will stick to vocabulary knowledge networks (Shanahan, 2019).

WHAT YOU CAN DO When choosing Tier 2 and Tier 3 words for instruction, think about words students need to know—words that are worth knowing—and how students will refer to and remember them. Nancy Hennessy recommends teaching and using Tier 2 and Tier 3 words in whole-group, small-group, and independent activities (Episode 157). And include them throughout the day—model how to use them, point them out in texts, and encourage students to use them in academic conversations, such as turn and talks, and in their writing. Kyair Butts, a middle school teacher from Baltimore, Maryland, says that decontextualized Tier 3 vocabulary can be tough for students to learn, but if they are learned in the context of texts that build students' knowledge, they are more likely to remember them (Episode 8).

Once you've started teaching words and students are becoming curious wordsmiths, have the class construct an interactive vocabulary wall and add words to it on an ongoing basis. That's right, have students construct it. We know that means it may not be Pinterest-worthy, but we promise, it's worth it. Why? Because the wall will not only be a teaching tool for you but also a point of pride for students as they add words from complex texts and rich discussions to it. Then students can manipulate the words, word parts, meanings, and more. Students might explore morphology and etymology, draw pictures inspired by the words, write their own definitions, and more (Shanahan, 2021). The possibilities are endless if you keep the focus on meaning-making.

CHECK OUT OUR PODCAST, EPISODE 156

"Science of Reading Beyond Phonics: Vocabulary Instruction" with Sean Morrisey In this episode, Sean Morrisey, a fifth-grade teacher from western New York, discusses the tiers of words, how to select words to teach using research-based approaches, and how to embed tiers of words into everyday language. If you're short on time, we discuss tiers of words in the first three minutes.

RELATED EPISODES

- **Episode 8:** "Kyair and Katie Talk REAL Teacher Talk!" with Kyair Butts and Katie Scotti
- **Episode 157:** "Science of Reading Beyond Phonics: Reading Comprehension Blueprint" with Nancy Hennessy

TEACHING TOOL

Interactive Vocabulary Wall

Fifth-grade teacher Sean Morrisey has his students create an interactive vocabulary wall at the beginning of the year and add to it as they learn Tier 2 and Tier 3 words. You can do the same! Sean's students learn words in a variety of contexts and, like all students, need repeated exposure to make them stick. From there, students post words to the wall as a visual reminder and reference. Students annotate right on the wall, underlining and circling word parts and noting where the word comes from.

One of Sean's favorite Tier 2 words to teach is *contract*, which students encounter in a variety of texts and contexts: muscles *contract*, illnesses are *contracted*, authors sign *contracts* for book deals. Think about the categories in which a word like *contract* could belong in an interactive vocabulary wall.

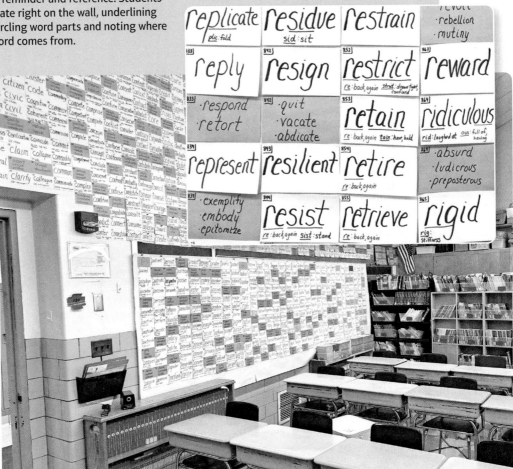

THE LITERACY 50—A Q&A HANDBOOK FOR TEACHERS

How do I choose words to teach?

ANSWER Choosing which words to teach can be tricky, and there's no right answer. There's not a magical, inarguable list of words, unfortunately. However, Tier 2 and Tier 3 words are usually great candidates.

Remember, vocabulary and knowledge are inextricable. Nancy Hennessy advises that before we choose words to teach, step back and think about the knowledge and skills we want students to take away from a text (Episode 157).

Consider a book that many teachers know and love: *Number the Stars* by Lois Lowry. What knowledge and skills would you want students to gain as they read that book? Perhaps knowledge related to World War II, the Holocaust, and mid-20th-century European geography. For skills, you may want students to gain a stronger understanding of point of view, symbolism, and plot—to the point where they can apply that understanding to other texts and their own writing.

Keeping in mind those big takeaways, ask yourself these questions when considering words to teach:

1. How useful is the word to understanding the text?
2. Is this a word that students will encounter in texts for this content area and others?
3. What's the general utility of this word?

(Beck, McKeown, & Kucan, 2002; Liben, 2013)

Choosing the right words to teach is important because they will support students' oral language, reading fluency, written expression, and reading comprehension.

WHAT YOU CAN DO When fifth-grade teacher Sean Morrisey was on the podcast, he read aloud an excerpt from *Number the Stars*, and we jotted down words from it that we would teach. The words we chose were important for several reasons. Some had multiple meanings, some had subtle differences in meaning, some transferred to content areas, some inspired morphology worthy of study, and so forth. Consider the following questions as you think about Tier 2 and Tier 3 words to teach. We've supplied examples from *Number the Stars* to support your understanding.

Which words will I teach explicitly and when? Teach *occupation* and *underground* before reading because they have multiple meanings. Students may become confused if they only know one meaning of each word as you or they read, which could hinder comprehension.

Teach *surrendered* and *declare* during reading and use context to support understanding. Students may also benefit from vocabulary routines before or after reading, such as identifying shades of meaning. (See Question 4.10 for more information.)

Which words will I define and move on from, and why? Quickly define the word *sabotage* during reading and keep going. Students need to know this word in the moment to understand what's happening. There's no need to spend a lot of time on this word because students will deepen their understanding from the text.

Which words' morphology and etymology will we explore? Explore morphology and etymology of the word *reciprocal*. Students will be able to apply the meaning of the prefix *re-* to understand this word and future words they read.

Which words should I encourage students to use in speaking and writing, and why? Choose high-utility Tier 2 words that students will encounter in content areas and in life, such as *declare* and *occupation*. Tier 2 words are important because they are used in multiple domains (Episode 156).

How will I spark students' curiosity about words? It's important for students to know what they don't know and have strategies in place to help (Shanahan, 2019). Hello, metacognition! So teach and model research-based vocabulary strategies, such as those we recommend in Question 4.10 (Kameenui, Carnine, & Freschi, 1982).

(For more on tiers of vocabulary, see Question 4.7.)

CHECK OUT OUR PODCAST, EPISODE 156

"Science of Reading Beyond Phonics: Vocabulary Instruction" with Sean Morrisey In this episode, Sean Morrisey discusses the tiers of words, how to select words to teach using research-based approaches, and how to best teach vocabulary. If you're short on time, listen from minute 3, where Sean shares vocabulary resources, to minute 19, where we choose words to teach from *Number the Stars*.

RELATED EPISODE

- **Episode 157:** "Science of Reading Beyond Phonics: Reading Comprehension Blueprint" with Nancy Hennessy

TEACHING TOOL

Choosing Tier 2 and Tier 3 Words

Use this planner to choose vocabulary words to teach. With the text as your guide, keep the big takeaways in mind for knowledge and skills as you evaluate vocabulary words. Consider what students have learned and which words are high-utility and necessary for understanding.

VOCABULARY PLANNER

Text: *Number the Stars* by Lois Lowry

What knowledge and skills do you want students to take away?

Knowledge	Skills
World War II and the Holocaust	Point of view
Various belief systems	Symbolism
Geography of Europe (Denmark and Germany) in 1943	Plot and story arc

Which words will you teach explicitly? When?	**Pre-teach** *occupation, underground* (multiple-meaning words) **Teach within text** *surrendered* (use context to support understanding) *declare* (teach shades of meaning: announce, declare, state, notify, publicize)
Which words will you define and move on? Why?	*sabotage* (tell the definition to understand what's happening quickly)
Which words will you have students explore in other ways (such as morphology, etymology, and/or context)?	**Teach morphology and etymology** *reciprocal* Prefix *re-* → again *reciprocal/reciprocate* → This word has Latin origins, meaning "returning the same way, alternating."
Which words will be integrated within speaking and writing? Why?	*declare* and *occupation* (likely to come up in other content-area texts as well as in real-life conversations)
How will you promote students' word curiosity?	• Will use a research-based vocabulary method that students can implement independently with practice. (See Question 4.9 for more info.) • Will model how to use vocabulary strategies to determine unknown words.

Download the "Vocabulary Planner."

How do I teach vocabulary? What are some research-based methods?

ANSWER Author Anita Archer says "Teach, don't ask" (2023). It's our job to explicitly teach students vocabulary words by providing opportunities to learn about words through rich texts and language experiences. Specifically, when teaching vocabulary, we should think about:

- Meanings
- Connection
- Usage
- Repetition
- Collaboration

(Shanahan, 2019)

Meanings

Going beyond a dictionary definition is necessary to build students' semantic networks, or concepts, of words (Stahl & Fairbanks, 1986). We can do that by having students connect meanings to objects, draw pictures, give performances, and compare and contrast words, to name a few methods (Kameenui, Carnine, & Freschi, 1982).

Connection

Encourage students to think about and identify relationships between words. This helps them learn new words and provides a strategy for use later, when learning words independently. One way to do that is to substitute simple words for more complex synonyms, such as *big* for *huge* or *gigantic* (Kameenui, Carnine, & Freschi, 1982). Another way to help students build connections is to ask them to link unknown words with known words and information (Stahl & Fairbanks, 1986).

Usage

Pronounce and have students pronounce words frequently because it supports their ability to retrieve meaning (Archer, 2023). Also, have students use vocabulary before, during, and after reading complex texts and in speaking and writing.

Repetition

Think about teaching vocabulary cyclically. In other words, revisit words you've taught to help them stick. By doing that, you help students build and strengthen semantic networks, or how concepts are related to each other. This helps with recall and retention.

> "You don't want to take 30 minutes to teach one word because you're just not going to have enough time to teach everything else during the day."
>
> **—SEAN MORRISEY, EPISODE 156**

Collaboration

Always engage students collaboratively in vocabulary work. One way to do that is to encourage curiosity around words. Another way is to teach vocabulary strategies that students can apply to any text, at any time. Most importantly, create a culture of word consciousness—help students notice what words they know and don't know—and help them find ways to learn words that work for them! (Shanahan, 2019).

WHAT YOU CAN DO

Three words: repetition, relevance, routine.

Repetition

- Teach vocabulary throughout the day, every day, because exposure matters (Stahl, 2005). That means if you're not your students only teacher, talk to your colleagues about the importance of word learning. Every teacher can support vocabulary learning.

- Explicitly teach students the meaning of words. Word learning happens when giving students a simple definition of the word, a context for the word, and opportunities for using the word (Episode 156).

Relevance

- Use Tier 2 and Tier 3 vocabulary when you speak, as much as possible. For example, in ELA, you might ask students to "analyze the plot structure," rather than "look at plot structure." In history, you might ask them to "dispute historical perspectives," rather than "talk to each other about historical perspectives."

- Choose words that matter, meaning those that students will find useful in many contexts. Also, teach the high-frequency words of mature language to boost their language abilities (Beck, McKeown, & Kucan, 2002).

Routine

- Teach word-learning strategies, such as those we highlight in Question 4.10. Students often learn vocabulary more quickly when they have familiar strategies to apply (Kamil, 2004).

- Have students read or read aloud narrative and informational complex, grade-level texts and promote wide reading in all grades and on topics students are studying. That builds and deepens knowledge and vocabulary. A win-win!

CHECK OUT OUR PODCAST, EPISODE 26

"Tim Shanahan Shares About Strategies and Knowledge-Building"
In this episode, Tim Shanahan discusses his blog post "Prior Knowledge, or He Isn't Going to Pick on the Baseball Study." He answers questions such as: Should we teach reading strategies? How important are building knowledge and vocabulary? What are reading skills vs. strategies? How frequent should strategy instruction occur in concert with building knowledge and vocabulary?

TEACHING TOOL

Five-Step Routine for Teaching Vocabulary

When we think about research-based vocabulary routines, one phrase comes to mind: explicit instruction. At a recent Reading League conference, we attended a session with Anita Archer, who shared an easy-to-implement and easy-to-replicate vocabulary routine. Although we've adapted it a bit, it aligns with what research tells us about effective instruction (Archer, 2023).

(Adapted from Anita Archer TRL 2023)

FIVE-STEP ROUTINE FOR TEACHING VOCABULARY	
1. Say the word, pronounce it with students, and explain its structure.	This is the word: *feature* Say it with me: *feature* Turn and say it out loud to a partner: *feature* Let's break it into parts: *fea-ture* Now put it together: *feature* I notice the *ea* vowel team is making the long *e* sound in *feature*. So I know that sometimes the vowel team *ea* says *e*. I don't hear the final *e* in feature. It's interesting that the *t* is making a /ch/ sound—*feature*. Did anyone else notice that?
2. Define the word and explore its meaning.	*Features* are interesting or important parts of something. Say and write the meaning in your vocabulary journal.
3. Make it tangible.	(Students are also learning about animal features in science class, so this ELA lesson will include photographs of animal features.) Let's look at some photographs of animal features.
4. Have students practice using the word.	In this example, the reader uses context through sentences, again focusing on animal features to connect to content students are learning about in science. "Many animals, birds, and people are carnivorous, which means they eat meat. You might be surprised to learn that some plants like the Venus flytrap and the pitcher plant are also carnivorous. These unusual plants have fascinating features to attract, trap, and kill their prey" (Episode 156).
5. Provide ongoing use.	Have students use the word *feature* in speaking and writing during our science unit. Add *feature* to our interactive vocabulary wall. Introduce another definition of *feature* during ELA class next week.

Download the "Five-Step Routine for Teaching Vocabulary" planner.

What strategies are helpful for teaching vocabulary?

ANSWER Students learn words in two ways:

1. Through explicit, systematic instruction on Tier 2 and Tier 3 words
2. By applying word learning strategies when encountering unfamiliar words

These are necessary for building students' vocabulary because we model strategic word analysis while building students' capacity to learn words independently. It's important to teach and model vocabulary strategies in context, including providing student-friendly definitions, teaching morphology and etymology, and modeling and using context clues (Episode 156). Once students have word-learning strategies in their mental toolbox, they can use those when encountering any unknown word. Big win! One caution though: Be sure to teach varied strategies because students need more than one way to access unfamiliar vocabulary (Archer, 2023; Beck, McKeown, & Kucan, 2002).

WHAT YOU CAN DO Remember, vocabulary learning shouldn't be left to chance. Here are some of our favorite tools to ensure that doesn't happen.

Frayer Model
Frayer models are tools to build and extend the meaning of words. This multipurpose tool can be used any time and in any content area. Students explore a word through "definition, characteristics, examples, and non-examples" (IRIS Center Peabody College Vanderbilt University, n.d.).

Semantic Maps
Semantic maps help students build vocabulary by linking a word to its meaning(s) and related words and concepts. Some examples of semantic maps include Venn diagrams, word webs, and timelines (Zorfass, Gray, & PowerUp WHAT WORKS, n.d.).

Vocabulary Continuum
Students place related words on a continuum based on meaning, or shades of meaning, to help them think about the subtle differences between them. They must consider each word and make decisions about its meaning, and then

> "So if I can put this word in context, we can practice a myriad of skills: context clues, inferencing, word roots... building it all in the context of the story which students already feel confident with because so much knowledge has been built."
>
> **—KYAIR BUTTS, EPISODE 8**

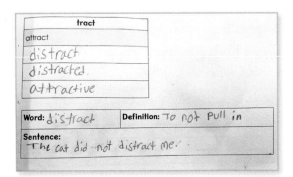

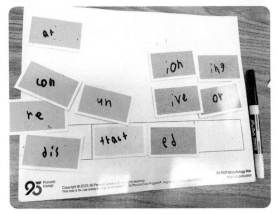

Students in Kory Jensen's fourth-grade class in Aurora, Colorado, explore morphemes to make words.

place it on the continuum, along with the other words, much like a number line in math. Give students a group of words and ask them to organize the words by the differences in meaning. We sometimes use paint swatches or light to dark markers on index cards to help students see shades of meaning (Episode 156).

Morpheme Matrices—and Etymology

Morpheme Matrices help students pinpoint morphemes in words—their prefixes, suffixes, roots, and bases, and connect to their etymologies, too (Frank, 2018). Students use a matrix to take apart words, create different words using those parts, and list new words they create. This tool helps students build a schema, or model, for morphemes by building words.

List-Group-Label

Students use List-Group-Label to organize and analyze related words. They brainstorm and list words related to a topic, group similar words by meaning, structure, or part of speech, and label groups according to how they're organized. This tool not only helps them categorize and organize words, but also activates prior knowledge and builds new knowledge (Reading Rockets, n.d.).

Odd One Out

Odd One Out inspires deep thought about words. Students are given several related words—except for one. Their challenge is to think about and discuss each word to determine which one doesn't belong. This game can be adapted for morphology instruction, too. Our fourth-grade teacher friend, Kory Jensen, chooses a word part, such as prefixes, and then chooses some words that contain that part, except for one. For example, Kory might choose the prefix *pre-* and the words *preheat*, *press*, *preschool*, and *prepay*. Then his students review to find the "odd one out": *press*. Although *press* begins with *pre-*, it's not a prefix meaning "before." This is a powerful way to connect and semantically map words, while building curiosity about vocabulary, morphology, and etymology (Episode 156).

TEACHING TOOL

Integrating Vocabulary Into Everyday Instruction

Here are examples of how fifth-grade teacher Sean Morrisey carries out Vocabulary Continuum and Odd One Out (Episode 156).

Vocabulary Continuum

Sean gives students a group of words and has them place them on a continuum to spur their thinking about subtle differences in meaning. Sometimes he uses chart paper, as shown here, and sometimes he has students go outside and use chalk to write the words on the pavement, or he hands out word cards and has students arrange themselves to show shades of meaning (Episode 156).

Odd One Out

Sean gives students a set of words and tells them, "One of these words is not like the others.... it's the odd one out!" He always provides students with enough time to say the words, think about them, discuss them, and determine the one that doesn't belong. This is a powerful way for students to drill down on the similarities and differences in word meanings (Episode 156).

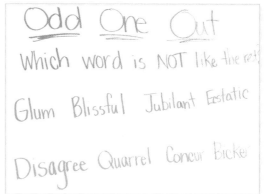

CHAPTER 5

COMPREHENSION

Comprehension is the act of making meaning from texts. It requires readers to use what they know and what they are learning to understand, interpret, and analyze what the author shares.

MELISSA'S STORY

When I was in my master's program to become a reading specialist, I was bombarded with information about traditional guided reading. My classmates and I learned how to assess students, assign them a reading level, group them, and give them books at their instructional level. It was a source of pride for us when students moved up a level.

I happened to run into author Doug Fisher at a conference around that time and asked him, "What do you think will be the next big change in literacy?" He quickly replied that it would be a move away from using leveled texts. At the time, I was skeptical about and surprised by his response. But now Lori and I are more skeptical of levels and leveled text. What does it really mean to be a Level M reader? What does it really mean for a text to be Level M? Studies report that leveling systems can be as reliable as flipping a coin!

I started to shift my thinking about what students need to help them comprehend texts. And, in turn, I started using more complex texts to help students build vocabulary and knowledge. Keep reading to learn all about how to teach reading comprehension!

Questions That Keep You Up at Night

5.1 Comprehension seems complicated to teach. In fact, can it even be taught? What does it take for a student to truly comprehend a text?

5.2 What are the best instructional practices to improve comprehension?

5.3 What is the role of knowledge in improving comprehension?

5.4 Is there a difference between activating knowledge and building knowledge? What does it mean for my teaching?

5.5 What is the difference between reading skills and reading strategies?

5.6 I keep hearing that we shouldn't be teaching reading comprehension strategies in isolation. What does that mean? What should I do instead?

5.7 Should I move away from using leveled texts? If so, what should I use instead?

5.8 What role does reading aloud play? What does a quality read-aloud look like?

5.9 What about sustained silent reading? I know there is a lot of pushback. Is there a place for it in the school day?

5.10 What are the best ways to assess a student's comprehension? Do you have suggestions?

Comprehension seems complicated to teach. In fact, can it even be taught? What does it take for a student to truly comprehend a text?

ANSWER Comprehension is complicated! But that doesn't mean we can't teach students to comprehend. Yes, we can teach reading comprehension... but not as an isolated skill or set of skills. Reading is a meaning-making process, involving the intersection of the reader, text, and activity (Kirby, 2003).

Reader

Author Anita Archer says, "There is no comprehension strategy powerful enough to compensate if a student cannot read the words" (2011). Students need to have word reading skills, such as phonological awareness, decoding, and sight recognition of familiar words, to decode words and read fluently so they have brain space for comprehending. Furthermore, language ability, background knowledge, motivation, and attention contribute to readers' understanding (Episode 179). Readers bring their unique set of prior knowledge to each text. And they need to tap into that knowledge to fill in information that the author may not provide.

Text

The features of a text play a crucial role in a reader's comprehension of that text. As readers engage with a text, three components help them make meaning: the wording of the text, idea units within the text that convey meaning, and the reader's ability to process information to gain meaning from the text. Every text is different in terms of subject matter, sentence structure, vocabulary, and coherence, which determines how easily a reader follows and makes sense of it (Episode 179).

Activity

Let's think about why we want students to comprehend a text. Of course we want them to understand and make meaning from it. However, comprehension goes beyond simply understanding. We also want students to have a purpose for reading and take action based on what they read. In 2020, researcher Nell Duke coined the term *compreaction*, blending *comprehension* and *action*. Hugh Catts said the purpose of reading is your "why." Are you reading an article to gather facts about a current event? Or maybe to learn about a topic to write a paper? (Episode 179). Doug Fisher proposed that the real purpose of comprehending is to take action in the world (Episode 158).

> "Comprehension is more than a product."
>
> —NANCY HENNESSY,
> EPISODE 157

WHAT YOU CAN DO If you notice students struggling with reading comprehension, you have to look at where they are with all the components that contribute to it, including phonemic awareness, phonics, and fluency. Assess them to peek under the hood, or into their reading brains, to see what's going on.

Continue to provide access to grade-level texts and tasks during Tier 1 instruction. Then for Tier 2 or Tier 3 instruction, teach what they need to fill in gaps. Form flexible small groups that meet their needs.

Importantly, continue to build vocabulary and knowledge for all students. Vocabulary and knowledge provide students with a way to access and understand what they are reading when they know what the words mean and have knowledge of the topic.

A Helpful Resource for Planning for Comprehension Instruction *Know Better, Do Better: Comprehension: Fueling the Reading Brain With Knowledge, Vocabulary, and Rich Language* by David and Meredith Liben contains practical strategies to implement in your classroom, such as questioning, close reading, and writing to understand, all centered on the text.

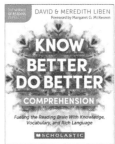

CHECK OUT OUR PODCAST, EPISODE 118

"Rethinking Reading Comprehension" with Hugh Catts In this episode, researcher Hugh Catts explains the complexities of the reader, the text, and the task as well as the role of prior knowledge in making meaning from texts.

RELATED EPISODES

- **Episode 158:** "Science of Reading Beyond Phonics: The Ultimate Goal of Reading" with Doug Fisher
- **Episode 179:** "The RAND Reading Model" with Hugh Catts

TEACHING TOOL

Steps for Comprehension Intervention

Here are some steps you can take to improve students' comprehension. Think about the components contributing to comprehension: phonemic awareness, phonics, and fluency. Then assess and teach as recommended below for Tier 2 or Tier 3 instruction while continuing with Tier 1 instruction.

Factor Contributing to Comprehension	If a student is having difficulty with...	Then (assess and teach Tier 2 or Tier 3)	Continue (Tier 1)
Fluency	fluent reading...	Assess oral-reading fluency.	Continue to have students read small chunks of grade-level texts and give read-alouds of grade-level texts that build knowledge on topics.
		Teach fluency targets such as accuracy, expression, and prosody.	
Phonics	regular and irregular spelled words or decoding and encoding skills...	Assess word recognition and phonics skills using nonsense-word lists.	Continue to teach phonics skills systematically and explicitly.
		Teach regular and irregular spelling patterns in a systematic sequence.	
Phonemic Awareness	basic phoneme segmenting, blending, and deletions...	Assess phonemic awareness and phonics.	Continue to teach phonemic awareness skills systematically and explicitly.
		Teach decoding skills.	

Download the "Steps for Comprehension Intervention" planner.

(Adapted from *Assessing Reading: Multiple Measures* by Consortium on Reaching Excellence in Education , Inc. (CORE))

What are the best instructional practices to improve comprehension?

ANSWER There's so much you can do to improve students' comprehension, such as building their knowledge and vocabulary, ensuring their sentence-level understanding, and teaching text structures, to name a few.

Build Knowledge and Vocabulary

Daniel Willingham says knowledge turns kids into great thinkers. He says, "Knowledge plays a role in all of the high-level cognitive processes, especially and including all the ones educators are really hoping that students are going to learn about and excel in at school... reasoning, problem-solving, creativity." Teaching vocabulary using multiple texts on the same topics and having students play with words help build knowledge (Episode 139).

> "Comprehension is more than a product."
>
> **—NANCY HENNESSY, EPISODE 157**

Ensure Sentence-Level Comprehension

Help students use strategies—such as rereading, summarizing, or looking up a vocabulary word—to engage with and make meaning from text. When students use strategies, they monitor their understanding—sentence by sentence, paragraph by paragraph. If they get stuck, encourage them to use strategies to solidify understanding before moving on (Hennessy, 2021). When rereading, they should ask themselves, "Where is the who or what and the do in the sentence?" (Hennessy & Salamone, 2024).

Teach Text Structures

There are two main types of text structures: narrative and informational. Narrative structures include story elements, such as characters, setting, plot, conflict, and resolution. Informational structures include cause and effect, compare and contrast, problem and solution, and sequencing, to name a few. Teaching structures helps students focus on the content and make meaning (Shanahan, 2019).

A Helpful Resource for Planning for Comprehension Instruction

Nancy Hennessy's *The Reading Comprehension Blueprint* outlines how to prepare for instruction by exploring the text(s) and unpacking the why—or purpose—for reading. Nancy explains evidence-based strategies and activities to consider before, during, and after reading that support constructing and monitoring comprehension.

WHAT YOU CAN DO There's so much to think about as you plan for systematic, explicit comprehension instruction. So here are our top five tips to make it more manageable.

1. Start comprehension instruction early, using complex texts. Even young students need opportunities to hear sophisticated language structures and build knowledge on topics (Duke, Ward, & Pearson, 2021; Willingham, 2006).

2. Consider why students are reading a text. Make the purpose and task clear to them.

3. Build background knowledge and vocabulary—both breadth and depth—through a variety of text types (Duke, Ward, & Pearson, 2021; Catts, 2021–2022). To reduce students' cognitive load, we should combine background knowledge and strategy instruction.

4. Teach text structures and reading strategies and use them to help students access complex texts. Think about which strategies, or combination of strategies, will help students access the text. One study found that the combination of main idea, text structure, and retelling helps students understand what they are reading (Peng et al., 2023).

5. Engage students in text through volume of reading, discussion, and writing (Shanahan & Lonigan, 2016).

CHECK OUT OUR PODCAST, EPISODE 157

"Science of Reading Beyond Phonics: Reading Comprehension Blueprint" with Nancy Hennessy

In this episode, Nancy Hennessy discusses the processes that underpin comprehension. Her Blueprint is a helpful graphic to understand how to plan for and think about reading comprehension.

RELATED EPISODE

- **Episode 155:** "Science of Reading Beyond Phonics: Language for Life" with Lyn Stone

TEACHING TOOL

Printable Bookmark

Print out this bookmark and keep it nearby as you plan for instruction in all content areas to support comprehension.

BOOKMARK: PLANNING FOR READING COMPREHENSION INSTRUCTION

Text: *Brave Irene* by William Steig (Grade 1)

What do I want students to know and be able to do after engaging with this text?	Know	Do
	The wind is a powerful force. The wind can help us. Authors use descriptive language to show feelings.	Act out a story scene to show understanding of descriptive language. Complete a narrative writing task using descriptive language (build knowledge and vocabulary for this during today's lesson).
What's the purpose for engaging with this text?	Build knowledge and vocabulary about the wind. This book is the third text students will encounter on this topic.	
What background knowledge and vocabulary are important for students to have? Are there other texts that would help build knowledge and vocabulary? If so, which ones?	Students have already read several texts on this topic: *The Boy Who Harnessed the Wind* by William Kamkwamba and Bryan Mealer, and a poem, "Feelings," by Aliki. They will be familiar with the concept of feelings and that people use the wind for power. Students may benefit from watching a video of a blizzard during this lesson.	
Which strategies—taught together—will help students access the text?	Students will pause at various stopping points during an interactive read-aloud to retell the story in chunks, answering the question, "What is happening right now?" As they do, they will respond by turning and talking and mix-pair-share. Teacher will record as students share responses on chart paper with the page number. Note: An effective strategy combination is main idea, text structure, and retell.	
What will students talk and write about to engage with the text and solidify understanding?	Students will work together to discuss, write, and act out a story scene to show understanding of figurative language.	

(Inspired by Grade 1 Module 3 *Wit & Wisdom* ELA texts and tasks.)

Download the "Bookmark: Planning for Reading Comprehension Instruction."

COMPREHENSION • QUESTION **5.3**

What is the role of knowledge in improving comprehension?

ANSWER Researcher and professor Susan Neuman asserts that "knowledge is comprehension in disguise" (2019). Knowledge and reading comprehension have a reciprocal relationship. Knowledge is sticky, like Velcro—and students need lots of it so when they encounter new texts, the learning sticks. Natalie Wexler, author of *The Knowledge Gap* and *The Writing Revolution*, underscores the necessity of building knowledge for comprehension. She says that knowledge sticks best to related knowledge, or familiar concepts. Think of it like "mental Velcro" (Episode 10; Adams, 2010–2011).

As students take in information, they organize new knowledge coherently. When we gain new knowledge, we organize it in our brains by connecting it to prior knowledge. We build on what we already know. If we do not have prior knowledge to connect to, that is okay. New information will wait for a forthcoming connection. Hugh Catts explains that our brains help us track new information or build on what we know through semantic networks that connect related concepts. Semantic networks build a foundation for meaning (Episode 118). (Read more about prior knowledge in Question 5.4.) When students build knowledge cumulatively and sequentially, they reduce their mental load (Willingham, 2006).

In the 1980s, researchers Recht and Leslie conducted the Baseball Study. Students of varying reading abilities read a text about baseball, moving figures around a board to reenact action described in the text. They found that prior knowledge about baseball made a huge difference in how much students comprehended the text. Kids who knew a lot about baseball, regardless of their reading abilities, outperformed more proficient readers. Many other studies show the importance of knowledge (Wexler, 2020; Kim et al., 2023).

Sonja Santelises, CEO of Baltimore City Schools, saw students' engagement increase and writing improve when teachers started implementing a knowledge building curriculum. She recalled stories of parents who were excited by the depth of their children's learning about topics such as the ocean. She also shared a fourth-grade teacher's observation: "They can't stop writing. And they write all the time" (Episode 22).

134   THE LITERACY 50—A Q&A HANDBOOK FOR TEACHERS

WHAT YOU CAN DO If we know that knowledge begets knowledge, then we should systematically and explicitly build students' knowledge and vocabulary on ELA and content-area topics. We can do that by having students read, or listen to different types of texts or watch media, on one topic for a sustained period of time (Episode 174). "Readers who have a strong knowledge of a particular topic, both in terms of quantity and quality of knowledge, are more able to comprehend a text than a similarly cohesive text for which they lack background knowledge," which is essential for building students' reading comprehension (Smith, Snow, Serry, & Hammond, 2021). With a knowledge-building curriculum, students gain deep knowledge from grade-level, complex texts—books, articles, poems, videos, and more. They then continue to build knowledge and vocabulary on topics within their grade and across grade bands—horizontally across a grade throughout one school year and vertically across grade levels throughout many school years.

"Out of all the texts in the world, why do we want to put this text in front of these students at this time?"

—ALFRED TATUM, EPISODE 68

This is why it's nearly impossible to replicate the effects of systematic knowledge building without the high-quality curricular materials, such as those vetted by the Knowledge Matters Campaign. We believe that teachers deserve strong curricular materials—and shouldn't have to spend their weekend or after-school hours writing or searching for them! However, we realize many teachers have curricular constraints and need to work with what they are provided.

CHECK OUT OUR PODCAST, EPISODE 139

"Knowledge and Comprehension" with Daniel Willingham and Barbara Davidson In this episode, we discuss knowledge as a critical component of reading comprehension with cognitive scientist Daniel Willingham and Executive Director of the Knowledge Matters Campaign Barbara Davidson.

RELATED EPISODES

- **Episode 10:** "Noticing the #KnowledgeGap" with Natalie Wexler
- **Episode 22:** "Leading Urgent Change in Baltimore" with Sonja Santelises
- **Episode 68:** "How Does Using a Text Analysis Toolkit Support Student Success?" with Quintin Bostic
- **Episode 118:** "Rethinking Reading Comprehension" with Hugh Catts
- **Episode 174:** "Unpacking the Knowledge Matters Review Tool" with Sue Pimentel and Barbara Davidson

TEACHING TOOL

Steps for Building Knowledge

Here are steps you can take to build knowledge, regardless of the materials you have available. Consider how to build on texts and topics already included in curricular materials by digging into the topics students already study (in ELA or other content areas, such as science, history, or health).

1. **Align** What topics do your students study? What texts do they use to explore these topics?

2. **Reflect** What can your students read, watch, or do to engage more deeply with the topic?

3. **Extend** What vocabulary is important to build knowledge on this topic? How can this information transfer to other topics or prepare students for forthcoming content? What experiences would be supportive of building additional knowledge?

ALIGN Consider topics and texts from ELA and content areas, such as science, history, or health.

What topics do your students study?	What texts do they use to explore these topics?
• Extreme weather and events • Extreme weather • How people survive in the wilderness • The resilience of the human spirit	*The River* by Gary Paulsen

REFLECT What can your students read, watch, or do to engage more deeply with the topic? Try to gather authentic texts, or real-world texts, such as videos, poems, articles, short stories, or books.

READ	WATCH
Books • *The River* by Gary Paulsen • *Camping and Wilderness Survival: The Ultimate Outdoors Book* by Paul Tawrell Articles • "National Geographic: Canadian Wilderness Animals" • "National Geographic: Canadian Wilderness Terrain"	• The Canadian Wilderness Bird's-Eye View • How to Fish Without a Line

DO
Work in teams to use the Survival Book to practice survival skills with limited tools and resources.

EXTEND

What vocabulary is important to build knowledge on this topic?	Survival, wilderness, types of plants/animals in Canadian wilderness, psychologist
How can this information transfer to other topics or prepare students for forthcoming content?	Informational writing strategies will transfer to other content areas
What experiences would build additional knowledge?	Camping, team-building field trip, hiking, nature walk, fishing

Download the "Steps for Building Knowledge" planner.

Is there a difference between activating knowledge and building knowledge? What does it mean for my teaching?

ANSWER Students come to us with prior knowledge and, once they're with us, they can build new knowledge.

Prior knowledge is the knowledge students possess, and they use it to help them understand what they read (Pappas, 2014). Activating it means teasing out what students already know about a topic and using it as a basis for teaching new content (Ferlazzo & Sypnieski, 2018). Prior knowledge provides connection points for learning. According to Daniel Willingham, "It allows you to chunk some information, which leaves more room in working memory to sort through the implications of a text" (2006). Furthermore, professor emeritus P. David Pearson claims the best predictor of comprehension is prior knowledge (2009). Some prior knowledge might be considered funds of knowledge, which students gain through daily routines and practices (Head Start Early Childhood Learning and Knowledge Center, 2023).

Think about it this way: Knowledge begets knowledge to create a continuous and connected cycle (Episode 139). For example, if students are reading texts about how food nourishes the body, you need to build their knowledge about food, the digestive system, and overall health. Likely, students will have some prior knowledge about those topics, as well as some gaps in their understanding. After all, it's rare for an elementary student to be able to explain the digestive process. How can we support them in understanding this topic and texts?

> "Kids are talking about WHAT they're learning in ELA during transitions and in content-area classes."
>
> —SETH BENJAMIN, EPISODE 104

Eliciting what students already know is an effective way to set the stage for learning. Then sharing texts with them about nourishing foods, food groups, body systems, and the digestive system ensures they have the knowledge they need to read and learn about the topic, and that new knowledge becomes prior knowledge. And the cycle continues.

WHAT YOU CAN DO Activating students' prior knowledge sets the stage for learning. It helps students make connections to new information, organize those connections, and extend learning. There are many ways to see what students know.

That said, activating prior knowledge only works if the knowledge being activated is accurate. If it isn't, it can harm comprehension (Catts, 2021–2022). Here are our top three tips for activating prior knowledge and building accurate knowledge on topics:

1. Use activities that are short and sweet and connect directly to the content of the lesson, such as our favorites on the next page.
2. Aim to build accurate knowledge and correct inaccurate knowledge quickly, in ELA and across the content areas.
3. Build deeper knowledge of topics through text sets on those topics, in ELA and across the content areas.

Seth Benjamin, a sixth-grade teacher from Skaneateles, New York, says that he and his teammates have "really made the entire knowledge-building program a part of what we do not just in ELA classrooms but social studies and science classrooms. Kids are talking about what they're learning in ELA during transitions and in content-area classes" (Episode 104). Isn't that every ELA teacher's dream?

Learning what students know, or think they know, helps us understand vocabulary needs, inconsistencies in understanding, and knowledge gaps. Continuing to build students' knowledge (so that it becomes their prior knowledge) supports their comprehension.

 CHECK OUT OUR PODCAST, EPISODE 10

"Noticing The #KnowledgeGap" with Natalie Wexler In this episode, Natalie Wexler, author of *The Knowledge Gap* and *The Writing Revolution*, shares a snapshot of research on knowledge-building. She deconstructs why and how we should build knowledge, making connections to classroom practice.

RELATED EPISODES

- **Episode 104:** "ELA Teacher + School Librarian = Knowledge-Building Dream Team" with Seth Benjamin and Kelly Gunderson
- **Episode 139:** "Knowledge and Comprehension" with Daniel Willingham and Barbara Davidson

Activities to Activate and Build Knowledge

Prep Texts

Prep texts are simpler texts that prepare students for a complex, forthcoming text. These texts might be texts that students can read at their independent levels or that students read repeatedly as a Readers' Theater script. Regardless of the type of text, the goal is to build knowledge, vocabulary, and confidence prior to reading a more difficult text. Note that these prep texts should not be a substitute for grade-level, complex text. This is especially helpful for multilingual learners, consider supplying multilingual learners with texts in their native language (Ferlazzo, 2014).

Download the "Prep Texts" planner.

What did I learn?	What vocabulary or terms seem important? Why?

TKWL Chart

This is a spin on the traditional KWL (Virginia Tech Center for Excellence in Teaching and Learning, n.d.). We used the KWL chart often to help students consider their prior knowledge, and realized that often they thought they knew something that they really… didn't. That's why this version includes **TK** = What I Think I Know, **W** = What I Want to Know, and **L** = What I Learned.

Before or at the beginning of a lesson, students fill in what they think they know (TK) and want to know (W) about the topic. During or at the end of the lesson, students add what they learned (L). At any point during the lesson, students can refer back to the what they think they know section and highlight or annotate what's accurate in their knowledge.

Download the "TKWL Chart."

What I Think I Know	What I Want to Know	What I Learned

Anticipation Guide

An anticipation guide provides students with several statements about the topic of the lesson. Before the lesson begins, students select if the statements are true or false, agree or disagree, yes or no. Choices could also be selected on a Likert Scale (a point rating) or sliding scale (i.e., strongly agree to strongly disagree). During and at the end of a lesson, students reflect on the accuracy of their original response, add to their thinking, and provide textual evidence and/or a page number to cite information (Reading Rockets, n.d.).

Download the "Anticipation Guide."

Before Reading		Statement	Was I correct? Evidence/Page #		During and After Reading
True	False		Yes	No	

What is the difference between reading skills and reading strategies?

ANSWER You might have heard the terms "reading skill" and "reading strategy" used interchangeably. Researcher and professor Peter Afflerbach and his colleagues surveyed educators about the meaning of those terms, and he says, "Ten people would give us ten different answers. They were all kind of related, but all different" (Episode 149).

Theodore Harris and Richard Hodges define the terms in *The Literacy Dictionary* (1995):

Skill: an acquired ability to perform well; proficiency.

Strategy: a systematic plan, consciously adapted and monitored, to improve one's performance in learning. Some strategies include summarizing, asking questions, and metacognition, or awareness of thought processes (Adler, 2001).

Reading comprehension strategies give students the tools they need to access text to become skilled readers (Shanahan, 2016). As you teach strategies and provide opportunities for students to practice, applying them becomes increasingly skillful. When a strategy becomes effortless and automatic, it becomes a skill. Good readers use strategies when needed, and can activate them over time (Episode 149).

> "It's a question of what you put in the foreground, the skills or the content. You've gotta put the content in the foreground and use the skills to help students get at that content."
>
> —NATALIE WEXLER, EPISODE 10

But don't forget, reading comprehension itself isn't an observable skill, like learning to ride a bike or swim. It relies on knowledge, vocabulary, and skills. It's simply not one skill to be mastered (Catts, 2021–2022; Liben & Liben, 2024). Texts, topics, and tasks are ever-changing, demanding that readers apply strategies as they encounter challenging words, concepts, and syntax and other text structures (Afflerbach, Pearson, & Paris, 2008). And don't forget that students are bringing prior knowledge to each text. Knowledge and vocabulary reduce the cognitive load as students use strategies to make sense of what they are reading (Peng et al., 2023).

WHAT YOU CAN DO Should we teach reading strategies? Yes, we should! As Natalie Wexler writes, "The question isn't whether to teach strategies—it's how to do it and when" (2023). There is synergy between applying strategies to and gaining knowledge from texts. It's a reciprocal relationship, and one is impossible without the other.

To access complex, grade-level texts, have students use strategies. Practicing strategies with complex texts allows students to become skillful meaning-makers. This will take effort on your students' part, engaging in productive struggle. Researcher Tim Shanahan says, "Strategy instruction emphasizes that you've got to comprehend, try to figure out what's important, and put more time into that part" (Episode 26).

We like to think about it like this: *Put the content of the text in the foreground and the strategies in the background.* Place an emphasis on learning from the texts. Reading a poem? Teach students to stop and jot questions. Reading a short story? Teach students to summarize chunks of text. Reading an article? Teach students to notice what they understand and don't understand. Do all that instead of teaching them to "master" reading comprehension strategies. Strategy instruction should be combined with background knowledge for maximum effectiveness (Peng et al., 2023).

When teaching strategies, less is more. While no one knows exactly how much strategy instruction students need, Tim Shanahan explains that students don't need isolated strategy instruction year after year after year (Episode 26).

To summarize: Less strategy instruction leads to more gains. Students should use strategies to access complex, grade-level texts. In other words, to learn stuff.

CHECK OUT OUR PODCAST, EPISODE 149

"Clarifying Differences Between Reading Skills and Reading Strategies" with Peter Afflerbach In this episode, researcher Peter Afflerbach clarifies the differences between reading skills and reading strategies, and the role of knowledge in reading.

RELATED EPISODE

- **Episode 26:** "Tim Shanahan Shares About Strategies and Knowledge-Building"
- **Episode 10:** "Noticing the #KnowledgeGap" with Natalie Wexler

I keep hearing that we shouldn't be teaching reading comprehension strategies in isolation. What does that mean? What should I do instead?

ANSWER Isolated strategy instruction, or instruction designed to help students to become experts at using a strategy such as finding the main idea or drawing a conclusion, doesn't necessarily improve reading (Peng et al., 2023). That's largely because we teachers have a habit of drilling students on strategies, using contrived texts—texts written for the sole purpose of teaching those strategies.

Strategies are tools that should be used for two main instructional purposes: developing reading skills and building content knowledge so our students can learn from text.

Strategy instruction is most effective when it's paired with building students' knowledge (Peng et al., 2023). Researcher Peter Afflerbach says that knowledge boosts strategy usage because it decreases the cognitive load for students and frees up brain space to gain information (Episode 149).

> "We don't read a text to check on our skills and our comprehension strategies.... The point of reading is to learn from it."
>
> —SUE PIMENTEL, EPISODE 37

While reading comprehension strategy instruction is effective, don't devote a lot of time and energy to it. More instruction doesn't necessarily mean more learning. The focus on strategy instruction should be "explicit and brief" (Willingham & Lovette, 2014). There's a limit to how much isolated strategy instruction students can grasp and apply.

When students practice strategies using contrived texts, the skills they gain don't necessarily transfer to more authentic, complex texts. We have learned that, for example, when a student can find the main idea in a text written for the purpose of finding the main idea, it does not mean he or she can do that for all texts, especially more complex texts.

WHAT YOU CAN DO Have your students read authentic, complex texts and use appropriate strategies to better understand them. Think about the text you're planning to use, what makes it complex, and what will help students make meaning from it.

Sue Pimentel spoke to us about what it means to keep complex text at the center of instruction. She reminded us that the point of reading is not to "check on our skills and our comprehension strategies" (Episode 37). It is to learn from what we read. That is what makes reading interesting and important!

You might be wondering how that works when the text is beyond a student's instructional reading level. Remember, our students can handle challenging texts. In fact, some studies have shown that when given the right support, our weakest readers can make more gains than our strongest readers with texts that are one-to-four grade levels *above* their instructional level (Brown, Mohr, Wilcox, & Barrett, 2017). For that to happen, though, they will continue to require instruction in vocabulary, syntax, text structure, and other aspects of language. Most students can read instructional-level texts fairly easily. To grow as readers, they need opportunities to engage with texts that contain complex structures and syntax, advanced vocabulary, and rich content (Shanahan, 2019).

Practicing strategies while reading authentic, complex texts is necessary because, according to Meredith Liben and Sue Pimentel, "Simpler texts, by their very nature, lack the features that make text complex, forcing students to artificially practice using strategies where there is no real need" (2018). So we shouldn't discontinue teaching our students comprehension strategies and how to use them. But we should provide a way for our students to access authentic, complex text. The planner on the next page will help.

CHECK OUT OUR PODCAST, EPISODE 37

"Placing Text at the Center of the ELA Classroom" with Meredith Liben and Sue Pimentel In this episode, authors of the Common Core State Standards (CCSS), Meredith Liben and Sue Pimentel, share the true intentions of the CCSS vs. the way they are interpreted. We consider what this means for assessment, especially "data-driven" instruction, and provide ideas for better ways to assess and track progress.

RELATED EPISODE

- **Episode 149:** "Clarifying Differences Between Reading Skills and Reading Strategies" with Peter Afflerbach

---

TEACHING TOOL

This planner will help you plan for instruction using complex, authentic texts.

1. Read the text.

2. As you do, jot down what makes the text complex.

3. Determine scaffolds that will help students make meaning from the text.

INSTRUCTION PLANNER

TEXT: *The Circulatory Story* by Mary K. Corcoran

What makes this text complex?	

Consider:
 	
• Sentence length
• Sentence structure
• Text structure
• Language conventions
• Vocabulary
• Topic/content
	• Vocabulary: Tier 3 words (e.g., *cell*, *vessel*, *platelet*)
	• Sentence structure:
	  ◆ dashes
	  ◆ parentheses
	  ◆ clauses
	• Topic/content: Students likely are lacking background knowledge about the circulatory system.

What will help students make meaning from this text?
 	
(pre-teaching select vocabulary, asking and answering questions, summarizing chunks of text, scaffolding knowledge building with additional texts, etc.)
	• Draw kids into the book's presentation, which is informative and fun.
	• Use page 6, which begins "It's time to find out...," for fluency practice (repeated readings) the week prior to familiarize students with the text and vocabulary.
	• Elicit prior knowledge with a TKWL (What You Think You Know, Want to Know, and Learned) chart.
	• Pre-teach AND review in context Tier 3 words students will encounter:
	  ◆ plasma
	  ◆ protein
	  ◆ components
	  ◆ erythrocyte or red blood cells
	  ◆ oxygen
	  ◆ hemoglobin
	• Chunk the text.
	• Stop and Jot: Use chart paper to visually capture how red blood cells travel through the body.

Download the "Instruction Planner."

Should I move away from using leveled texts? If so, what should I use instead?

ANSWER When we assess students and assign them a reading level and then use texts at that level to teach them, it does not improve their reading and can have long-term negative effects. There is no research to support differentiating reading instruction by text levels (Episode 143). Holding onto practices that are unsupported by research, such as using leveled texts for instruction, instead of shifting to new ones, such as using complex texts, can cause "a balanced literacy hangover," says Brent Conway, assistant superintendent of Pentucket Regional School District in West Newbury, Massachusetts.

Author and professor Alfred Tatum (2017) said, "Leveled texts lead to leveled lives," which makes us think about students remaining at specific levels, or moving through them at a snail's pace, throughout their school careers. Furthermore, students who are assigned higher level texts have regular access to rich content and learn more vocabulary, gain more knowledge, and learn how to navigate more complex sentence structures. On the other hand, students who are assigned lower-level texts don't get those opportunities and usually end up reading only lower-level texts, year after year. This is called the Matthew Effect, where the rich get richer and the poor get poorer, and it creates an achievement gap (Stanovich, 1986).

Most students can read instructional-level texts fairly easily. So it is critical to help them move away from those texts and read complex, grade-level texts instead. They need opportunities to engage with texts that contain varied sentence structures, rich vocabulary, and intricate content (Shanahan, 2019). You can't use simple text if you want students to become proficient at reading complex text! (Episode 103).

> "Holding onto practices that are unsupported by research, such as using leveled texts for instruction, instead of shifting to new ones, such as using complex texts, can cause 'a balanced literacy hangover.'"
>
> —BRENT CONWAY, EPISODE 103

WHAT YOU CAN DO When you're focusing on comprehension, make sure the texts students are reading are complex and at grade level to give students access to knowledge and ideas. Literacy researcher and educator Tim Shanahan says, "The point shouldn't be to place students in books easy enough to ensure good reading, but to provide enough scaffolding to allow them to read harder books successfully" (2014). Scaffolding techniques, such as defining vocabulary words in context or repeated readings, allow students to access texts that otherwise may have been challenging. But don't provide so many scaffolds that you diminish the challenge that will push them to become better readers.

You might be wondering whether to use complex, grade-level text if students are still learning to decode. The answer is yes! But provide access to those texts through read-alouds. Meredith Liben explains, "Foundational skills... work in concert with the reading comprehension side of the standards. Even in kindergarten, it's mostly through oral comprehension, students get to grapple with complex ideas... don't withhold the good stuff..." (Episode 37). The "good stuff," as Meredith puts it, are the ideas, vocabulary, structure, syntax, and other elements that make a text complex and, therefore, worth reading.

If students are just learning to decode, use decodable texts to help them practice taught sound-spelling patterns. Do not use texts that contain too many words that they will not be able to decode because they will hit a frustration point. However, once your students are reading accurately at an appropriate rate, it's time to let them grapple with more complex, grade-level text that will build their knowledge and vocabulary.

 CHECK OUT OUR PODCAST, EPISODE 103

"From Workshop Model to Reading Science in Pentucket" with Brent Conway and Jen Hogan

In this episode, Brent Conway and Jen Hogan, leaders from Massachusetts's Pentucket Regional School District, explain why they made the move from balanced literacy (workshop model) to reading science (building knowledge and more).

RELATED EPISODES

- **Episode 37:** "Placing Text at the Center of the ELA Classroom" with Meredith Liben and Sue Pimentel
- **Episode 143:** "Maximizing Small-Group Reading Instruction" with Kristin Conradi Smith, Steven Amendum, and Tamara Williams

Level-Headed Uses for Leveled Texts

Do you have tubs full of leveled texts? Are you wondering what to do with them? Don't throw them away! Many teachers are organizing their leveled texts by topic instead of level. They're aligning them to topics in their ELA, social studies, and science curricula, such as "body systems" or "the Revolutionary War." Text sets, or collections of texts focused on a specific topic, help students develop rich vocabulary and deepen their knowledge.

Think about the topics your students are studying in ELA, science, social studies, or health (and other content areas too—like art, music, or physical education). Then take stock of your leveled texts by asking yourself these questions:

- Which texts align to the topics in content-area classes?
- How can students build or continue to build their knowledge base about the topic with repurposed leveled texts?

TOPIC-ALIGNED TEXTS LEVELED TEXTS BY TOPIC

Content Area	Topic of Study	Texts Aligning with Topics
ELA	Extreme Weather	*Canyon Mystery* *Earthquakes* *Tsunamis: Mighty Ocean Waves* *The Big Snow*
Science	Animals in the Wild	*Not Too Cold for a Polar Bear* *Animal Adaptations* *All About Koalas* *Why Do Wolves Howl?* *Surprising Animal Senses* *Snake Myths* *Hang on, Baby Monkey*
	The Sea	*Giants of the Sea* *The Amazing Undersea Food Web*
History	Westward Expansion	*1849: The California Gold Rush* *The Great Land Rush* *Westward Journey*
Health	Healthy Habits	*Healthy Me* *Fall Foods* *The Food Groups* *The Food I Eat* *Food Idioms* *Food Trucks* *A Rainbow of Food*

Download the "Topic-Aligned Texts Leveled by Topic" planner.

What role does reading aloud play?
What does a quality read-aloud look like?

ANSWER The benefits of read-alouds to literacy learning have long been proven by research (Håland, Hoem, & McTigue, 2021). Although they are most commonly practiced in preschool and elementary classrooms, read-alouds are invaluable to students at all grade levels (Ness, 2024). Furthermore, Elsa Cárdenas-Hagan says they are an effective way to give students access to complex text, expand listening comprehension, world knowledge, and background knowledge (Episode 119).

The terms read-aloud and an interactive read-aloud are often used interchangeably (Ness, 2024). We chose to use the term read-aloud to define the experience of students listening to a proficient reader model fluent reading, as well as discuss, confirm, and extend comprehension.

Some of our best teacher memories are the times we spent reading aloud to our students! We built knowledge about countless topics with Ms. Frizzle on the *Magic School Bus*, walked beside Elijah as he came of age in *Elijah of Buxton*, and battled the wilderness with Buck in *The Call of the Wild*. Students listened as we read, building their language comprehension skills.

Author of *Read Alouds for All Learners*, Molly Ness, says, "The purpose [for read-alouds] is language comprehension. We are giving them exposure to background knowledge, activating their purposes for reading… opening the door for juicy conversations by sharing a common text" (Episode 170).

CHECK OUT OUR PODCAST, EPISODE 170

"All About Read-Alouds" with Molly Ness In this episode, researcher and educator Molly Ness explains how to intentionally plan for read-alouds and why they're so important in every grade and every content area.

RELATED EPISODE

- **Episode 119:** "How Reading Science Works for English Learners" with Elsa Cárdenas-Hagan

There are many benefits to read-alouds, including:

- Building knowledge and vocabulary to support students' literacy, content-area, and social-emotional development (Biemiller, 2003).
- Allowing students opportunities to hear fluent reading of complex, grade-level text that students would not likely be able to read independently.
- Helping students understand the purpose of reading—or why we read (Price, van Kleeck, & Huberty, 2009).

> "Before age 13, students' listening comprehension surpasses their reading comprehension. Read-alouds are a way to access complex texts before students can read them independently."
>
> —MOLLY NESS, EPISODE 170

Ideally, teachers ask students to discuss the text before, during, and after reading to meaning-make together (Beck & McKeown, 2001). They draw attention to text by unpacking ideas and vocabulary with students (Ness, 2024). The teacher guides students through the book—questioning, wondering about, and making sense of it—alongside students.

Read-alouds are not an activity to do when there's extra time. They are a must-do activity, a necessary part of classroom instruction. How can we integrate read-alouds into our daily instructional routines?

WHAT YOU CAN DO As you plan for read-alouds, consider the following points.

Text Selection

- Choose high-quality texts, including complex, grade-level narrative and informational texts.
- Continue to build knowledge and vocabulary on topics students are learning about in ELA, science, history, health, and other content areas (Lennox, 2013).

Meaningful Interactions

- Ask text-dependent questions. Initial questions help ensure a base level understanding, while follow-up questions go deeper into the text (Beck & McKeown, 2001).
- Discuss the text's big ideas and make sense of them together. Use sentence frames such as "I notice..." and "I wonder..." to support inquiry.

Background Knowledge, Vocabulary, and Inferencing Skills

- Find out what students know, or think they know, about a topic. Then select texts that support vocabulary and knowledge-building (Kaefer, 2020).
- Deliberately plan for vocabulary instruction. Pre-teach new words, have students explore words in context, and explicitly teach Tier 2 and Tier 3 words. Repetition is key (Lennox, 2013).

What about sustained silent reading? I know there is a lot of pushback. Is there a place for it in the school day?

ANSWER The best way to maximize instructional time is with instruction (Episode 143; Conradi Smith et al., 2022). Instructional time allows us to explicitly teach so students can practice and solidify learning.

After reviewing several hundred studies, the National Reading Panel did not find research supporting the use of instructional time for silent independent reading, also known as sustained silent reading or DEAR time. Although many studies have shown that good readers read more than poor readers, it is likely that good readers prefer to read more. When we can do something well, we are motivated to continue doing it (Shanahan, 2016). Being able to read is no different (Episode 120). We asked the CEO of UnboundEd, Lacey Robinson, about her popular quote from the documentary podcast, "Sold a Story:" "Everybody has a right to learn to read and write... I don't want them to love [it]. I want them to know how to do it. Love comes later." Lacey explains she's skeptical about struggling readers finding enjoyment in extended periods of time spent independently reading (Episode 144). If we want kids to love reading, we should spend instructional time teaching them to read well.

> "A series of texts on a topic will improve students' vocabulary and knowledge."
>
> **—DAVID LIBEN, EPISODE 91**

Although there isn't research supporting traditional sustained silent reading, there is research supporting reading volume, which is the amount of time children spend reading and the number of words they read (Liben & Liben, 2024). For students reading fluently, a volume of reading has benefits. Reading volume is how we build knowledge and vocabulary—by reading text sets about topics students are learning about. If students are still working on foundational skills, such as decoding accuracy, independent silent reading may not be the most efficient use of time.

WHAT YOU CAN DO So how can we increase students' reading volume? Consider text sets and full-length texts.

Text Sets

Text sets are a series of texts on a topic (Cervetti, Wright, & Hwang, 2016). To create one, gather texts of varying readability on a topic students are studying in ELA or in a content area. Yes, that includes multimedia, articles, poems, and more (Episode 91). Have students read them not only during subject blocks, but also during transition times, at centers or stations, or for homework.

You might be wondering about the difference between topics and themes. With topics, students read multiple texts over time that build on related knowledge and vocabulary, which helps learning stick. With themes, students tend to skip around and move quickly from one topic to the next. As such, they are less likely to build knowledge and vocabulary in a coherent way. Examples of topics include the Revolutionary War and extreme weather, while themes might include friendship and communities (Pimentel, Liben, & Liben, 2023).

Full-Length Texts

Like text sets, full-length texts support learning by connecting to a topic that students are studying in ELA or a content area. They can be fiction, nonfiction, or poetry. For example, if students are studying the middle ages, they might read an informational text about the class system, or a book of poems or novel set in medieval times.

Regardless of text type, reading full-length texts connected to a topic builds, deepens, and extends knowledge and vocabulary, and helps students comprehend even more complex texts.

CHECK OUT OUR PODCAST, EPISODE 91

"Improving Reading for Older Students, Part 2" with David Liben
In this episode, reading expert David Liben discusses independent reading and how to make it more effective through volume of reading.

RELATED EPISODES

- **Episode 120:** "Research-Based Routines for Developing Decoding Skills" with Julia Lindsey
- **Episode 143:** "Maximizing Small-Group Reading Instruction" with Kristin Conradi Smith, Steven Amendum, and Tamara Williams
- **Episode 144:** "The Science of Reading as More Than a Pendulum Swing" with Lacey Robinson and Margaret Goldberg

What are the best ways to assess a student's comprehension? Do you have suggestions?

ANSWER Before we talk about the best ways to assess comprehension, consider what might be getting in the way of a student being able to comprehend a text. The student's ability to read the text fluently, his or her vocabulary and prior knowledge, the demands of the text, the assigned task, and the instructional context all influence comprehension. Assessments of reading comprehension often ask students questions, such as "What is the main idea of this text?" But that type of question cannot be measured accurately in isolation because questions that aim to isolate skills cannot be repeated from text to text or task to task, since there are so many reasons why a student may or may not be able to find the main idea of a particular text.

If you're reading this thinking, standards-based grading attempts to measure reading comprehension "skills" in isolation... you're right. We don't recommend using standards-based grading for reading comprehension for this very reason.

E.D. Hirsch, Jr., Chairperson of the Core Knowledge Foundation, says, "Reading tests are actually knowledge tests in disguise" (2016). What if a reading test included content-rich passages on topics students learned about from instruction? This is far more sensible than holding students accountable for knowledge, vocabulary, and syntax they learned outside of the school day, rather than during the school day (Catts, 2021–2022).

In short, let's test what we teach. And let's teach content-rich topics that build knowledge and vocabulary. Let's help students access information on those topics from texts by providing explicit strategy instruction. Let's connect reading to speaking and writing. Let's use an integrated approach to teach and test skills and knowledge.

WHAT YOU CAN DO What is the easiest way to approach comprehension assessments? Stay within your curriculum topics.

During an episode on innovative assessments, we talked with members of the Louisiana Department of Education team. They said, "We know the importance of building knowledge in reading comprehension, we know that's one of the biggest roadblocks for understanding." That team is working to create equitable assessments by only using reading passages that relate to topics students have learned about within the curriculum (Episode 124).

In real life, students will be asked to show what they know and what they can do. So let's mimic that in assessments by considering the authenticity of tasks connected to knowledge and skills taught. Informal classroom-based assessment can and should inform instruction. Each lesson should include a check for understanding connected to the content and goals of the lesson. The lesson assessments should build to a task illuminating what students have been learning about for a significant period of time. And in between there should be assessments to measure that progress.

Remember, test what you've taught, including necessary skills, knowledge, and understanding of content (Episode 124).

Dos and Don'ts of Reading Comprehension Assessment

Here are some tips for the best ways to assess students' comprehension. Use this handy chart as you consider what to assess—and what not to assess.

Do	Don't
Stay within the curriculum and assess what is taught.	Use standards-based grading.
Use discussion and writing as measures of comprehension.	Use comprehension assessments outside of the curriculum as a measure of learning.
Consider what else might be getting in the way (fluency, gaps in foundational skills, etc.).	Use comprehension assessments as a way to predict future comprehension.

CHECK OUT OUR PODCAST, EPISODE 124

"Innovative Assessment with the Louisiana Assessment Team" In this episode, representatives from the Louisiana Department of Education tell how they are revising assessments across the state to align to what students are learning. It's revolutionary!

CONCLUSION

There was a moment during our science of reading learning journeys that we will always remember. We were in a classroom, sitting next to each other, and reading *Wit & Wisdom* ELA's research base, which cites research by Marilyn Jager Adams, Lily Wong Fillmore, Tim Shanahan, and Julie Washington. We turned to each other and said some version of: "Why haven't we ever read this research before? We are certified reading specialists... Why is this the first time we're seeing this information? And why is it SO different from what we learned?"

That moment in time occurred over halfway through our teaching careers. If we didn't know about this research, then others must not either. That memory drives us to continue to learn, grow, and advocate for research-based reading instructional practices. This big change starts with curiosity, an openness to learning, and willingness to put students first.

When we asked Sonja Santelises, CEO of Baltimore City Public Schools, for a piece of advice, she said, "really immerse yourself in the reading science and the writing science and how kids learn. I have yet to meet a teacher who when confronted with what we know, what has been reaffirmed, and what is clear about ... the need for all of the different components, be it phonics or phonemic awareness or vocabulary development, who don't say that their everyday teaching is better because of it" (Episode 22).

Kareem Weaver shared some sage wisdom with us: "We need courage for people to say, 'I'm learning. And there's no shame in not knowing something that you don't know. There's no shame'" (Episode 112).

We will keep asking questions. We will continue to connect research and practical application. And we hope you will, too. Together, we can do this!

Keep in touch!

Check out our website where you can sign up for our email list: literacypodcast.com. Listen to our podcast on your favorite podcast platform, such as Apple Podcasts or Spotify.

Connect with us on social media:

- Follow us on Facebook: Melissa and Lori Love Literacy
- Join our Facebook Group: Melissa and Lori Love Literacy Podcast
- Follow us on Instagram and X/Twitter: @literacypodcast

REFERENCES

Achieve the Core. (n.d.). *Knowledge & vocabulary (K–2).*

Adams, M. J. (2010–2011, Winter). Advancing our students' language and literacy: The challenge of complex texts. *American Federation of Teachers.* https://www.aft.org/sites/default/files/Adams.pdf

Adler, C. R. (Ed.) (2001). *Put reading first: The research building blocks for teaching children to read.* National Institute for Literacy. https://lincs.ed.gov/publications/pdf/PRFbooklet.pdf

Afflerbach, P., Pearson, P. D., & Paris, S. G. (2008). Clarifying differences between reading skills and reading strategies. *The Reading Teacher, 61*(5), 364–373.

Archer, A. (2023, October 2–4). *Getting them all engaged: The power of active participation.* The 7th Annual Reading League 2023 Convention.

Archer, A. L., & Hughes, C. A. (2011). *Explicit instruction: Effective and efficient teaching.* The Guilford Press.

Beck, I. L., & McKeown, M. G. (1985). Teaching vocabulary: Making the instruction fit the goal. *Educational Perspectives,* 23.

Beck, I. L., & McKeown, M. G. (2001). Text talk: Capturing the benefits of read-aloud experiences for young children. *The Reading Teacher, 55*(1), 10–20.

Beck, I. L., McKeown, M. G., & Kucan, L. (2002). *Bringing words to life: Robust vocabulary instruction.* The Guilford Press.

Biemiller, A. (2003, Spring). Oral comprehension sets the ceiling on reading comprehension. *American Federation of Teachers.* https://www.aft.org/ae/spring2003/biemiller

Bottari, M. (2020, November 4). *Why make the switch? Transitioning from word walls to sound walls.* Heggerty. https://heggerty.org/resources/blog-post/sound-walls

Boyer, N., & Ehri, L. C. (2011). Contribution of phonemic segmentation instruction with letters and articulation pictures to word reading and spelling in beginners. *Scientific Studies of Reading, 15*(5), 440–470.

Brady, S. (2020). A 2020 perspective on research findings on alphabetics (phoneme awareness and phonics): Implications for instruction (expanded version). *The Reading League Journal.*

Brown, L. T., Mohr, K. A. J., Wilcox B. R., & Barrett, T. S. (2017). The effects of dyad reading and text difficulty on third-graders' reading achievement. *The Journal of Educational Research, 111*(5), 541–553.

Catts, H. (2021–2022, Winter). Rethinking how to promote reading comprehension. *American Federation of Teachers.* https://www.aft.org/ae/winter2021-2022/catts

Cervetti, G. N., Wright, T. S., & Hwang, H. (2016). Conceptual coherence, comprehension, and vocabulary acquisition: A knowledge effect? *Reading and Writing, 29,* 761–779.

Chard, D. J., & Dickson, S. V. (1999). Phonological awareness: Instructional and assessment guidelines. *Reading Rockets.*

Clemens, N., Solari, E., Kearns, D. M., Fien, H., Nelson, N. J., Stelega, M., & Hoeft, F. (2021). They say you can do phonemic awareness instruction "in the dark," but should you? A critical evaluation of the trend toward advanced phonemic awareness training.

Colenbrander, D., Kohnen, S., Beyersmann, E., Robidoux, S., Wegener, S., Arrow, T., Nation, K., & Castles, A. (2022). Teaching children to read irregular words: A comparison of three instructional methods. *Scientific Studies of Reading, 26*(6), 545–564.

Colenbrander, D., Wang, H. C., Arrow, T., & Castles, A. (2020). Teaching irregular words: What we know, what we don't know, and where we can go from here. *Educational and Developmental Psychologist, 37*(2), 97–104.

Conrad, N. J., Kennedy, K., Saoud, W., Scallion, L., & Hanusiak, L. (2019). Establishing word representations through reading and spelling: Comparing degree of orthographic learning. *Journal of Research in Reading, 42*(1), 162–177.

Conradi Smith, K., Amendum, S. J., & Williams, T. W. (2022). Maximizing small-group reading instruction. *The Reading Teacher, 76*(3), 348–356.

CORE Literacy Library. (2018). *Assessing reading: Multiple measures* (2nd ed.). Arena Press.

Cunningham, A. E., & Stanovich, K. E. (2001). What reading does for the mind. *Journal of Direct Instruction, 1*(2), 137–149.

Dahlgren, M. (2020, May 20). *Implementing a sound wall: Because we need to distinguish between sounds and letters.* EDVIEW360.

Diamond, L. (2023, June). *Small-group reading instruction and mastery learning: The missing practices for effective and equitable foundational skills instruction.* Center for Collaborative Classroom.

Duke, N. K., Lindsey, J. B., & Wise, C. N. (2023). Feeding two birds with one hand: Instructional simultaneity in early literacy education. In S. Q. Cabell, S. B. Neuman, and N. Patton Terry (Eds.), *Handbook on the science of early literacy.* The Guilford Press.

Duke, N. K., Ward, A. E., & Pearson, P. D. (2021). The science of reading comprehension instruction. *The Reading Teacher, 74*(6), 663–672.

Ehri, L. C. (1995). Phases of development in learning to read words by sight. *Journal of Research in Reading, 18*(2), 116–125.

Ehri, L. C. (2013). Orthographic mapping in the acquisition of sight word reading, spelling memory, and vocabulary learning. *Scientific Studies of Reading, 18*(1), 5–21.

Ehri, L. C., & Roberts, T. (2006). The roots of learning to read and write: Acquisition of letters and phonemic awareness. In D. K. Dickinson & S. B. Neuman (Eds.), *Handbook of early literacy research.* The Guilford Press.

Eide, D. (2012). *Uncovering the logic of English.* Logic of English, Inc.

Erbeli, F., Rice, M., Xu, Y., Bishop, M. E., & Goodrich, J. M. (2024.) A meta-analysis on the optimal cumulative dosage of early phonemic awareness instruction. *Scientific Studies of Reading.*

Farrell, L., & Hunter, M. (2021, October 16). *Using decodable and leveled readers appropriately.* [Video]. YouTube.

Ferlazzo, L. (2014, November 16). The best places to get the "same" text written for different levels. https://larryferlazzo.edublogs.org/2014/11/16/the-best-places-to-get-the-same-text-written-for-different-levels

Ferlazzo, L., & Sypnieski, K. H. (2018, May 28). *Activating prior knowledge with English language learners.* Edutopia.

Firth, J., Rivers, I., & Boyle, J. (2021). A systematic review of interleaving as a concept learning strategy. *Review of Education, 9*(2), 642–684.

Foorman, B., Beyler, N., Borradaile, K., Coyne, M., Denton, C. A., Dimino, J., Furgeson, J., Hayes, L., Henke, J., Justice, L., Keating, B., Lewis, W., Sattar, S., Streke, A., Wagner, R., & Wissel, S. (2016). Foundational skills to support reading for understanding in kindergarten through 3rd grade (NCEE 2016-4008). National Center for Education Evaluation and Regional Assistance (NCEE), Institute of Education Sciences, U.S. Department of Education.

Frank, M. (2018). Morpheme matrices: Sequential or standalone lessons for assembling common prefixes, Latin roots, Greek forms, and suffixes. OER Commons.

Gatlin-Nash, B. (2023). Language variation & literacy: Where do we go from here? *The Reading League's Annual Conference.*

Genry, J. R., & Ouellette, G. P. (2019). *Brain words: How the science of reading informs teaching.* Routledge.

Ginsberg, M. (2019). The 411 on 4 types of reading errors. *Reading Simplified.* https://readingsimplified.com/4-types-reading-errors

Graves, M. F., & Watts-Taffe, S. (2002). The place of word consciousness in a research-based vocabulary program.

Håland, A., Hoem, T. F., & McTigue, E. M. (2021). The quantity and quality of teachers' self-perceptions of read-aloud practices in Norwegian first-grade classrooms. *Early Childhood Education Journal, 49,* 1–14.

Hall, M. S., & Burns, M. K. (2018). Meta-analysis of targeted small group reading interventions. *Journal of School Psychology, 66,* 54–66.

Hanford, E. (2018). *Hard words: Why aren't kids being taught to read?* APM Reports.

Harris, T., & Hodges, R. (1995). *The literacy dictionary: The vocabulary of reading and writing*. International Reading Association.

Hasbrouck, J., & Tindal, G. (2017). *An update to compiled ORF norms* (Technical Report No. 1702). Behavioral Research and Teaching, University of Oregon.

Head Start Early Childhood Learning and Knowledge Center. (2023). *Funds of Knowledge Video*. U.S. Department of Health & Human Services.

Heilman, A. W., Blair, T. R., & Rupley, W. R. (1998). *Principles and practices of teaching reading*. Merrill/Prentice-Hall.

Hennessy, N. L. (2021). *The reading comprehension blueprint: Helping students make meaning from text*. Brookes.

Hennessy, N. L., & Salamone, J. A. (2024). *The reading comprehension blueprint activity book: A practice & planning guide for teachers*. Brookes.

Hirsch, E. D. (2016). *Why knowledge matters: Rescuing our children from failed educational theories*. Harvard Education Press.

Honig, B., Diamond, L., & Gutlohn L. (2018). *Teaching reading sourcebook*. Core Literacy Library.

International Literacy Association. (2018). *Literacy leadership brief: reading fluently does not mean reading fast*. https://www.literacyworldwide.org/docs/default-source/where-we-stand/ila-reading-fluently-does-not-mean-reading-fast.pdf

Iowa Department of Education. (2023, June 13). *This school upped its kindergarten literacy proficiency rates by double digits. How?* Official State of Iowa Website.

IRIS Center Peabody College Vanderbilt University. (n.d.). *Building vocabulary and conceptual knowledge using the Frayer model*. https://iris.peabody.vanderbilt.edu/module/sec-rdng/cresource/q2/p07/#content

Jones, C. D., Clark, S. K., & Reutzel, D. R. (2012). Enhancing alphabet knowledge instruction: Research implications and practical strategies for early childhood educators. *Early Childhood Education Journal, 41*(2), 81–89.

Kaefer, T. (2020). When did you learn it? How background knowledge impacts attention and comprehension in read-aloud activities. *Reading Research Quarterly, 55*(S1), 173–183.

Kameenui, E. J., Carnine, D. W., & Freschi, R. (1982). Effects of text construction and instructional procedures for teaching word meanings on comprehension and recall. *Reading Research Quarterly, 17*(3), 367–388.

Kamil, M. L. (2004). Vocabulary and comprehension instruction: Summary and implications of the National Reading Panel finding. In P. McCardle and V. Chhabra (Eds.), *The voice of evidence in reading and research*. Brookes.

Kemeny, L. (2023). *7 mighty moves: Research-backed, classroom-tested strategies to ensure K-to-3 reading success*. Scholastic.

Kilpatrick, D. (2016). *Equipped for reading success: A comprehensive, step-by-step program for developing phoneme awareness and fluent word recognition*. Casey & Kirsch Publishers.

Kim, J. S., Burkhauser, M. A., Relyea, J. E., Gilbert, J. B., Scherer, E., Fitzgerald, J., Mosher, D., & McIntyre, S. (2023). A longitudinal randomized trial of a sustained content literacy intervention from first to second grade: Transfer effects on students' reading comprehension. *Journal of Educational Psychology*.

Kirby, S. N. (2003). *Developing an R&D program to improve reading comprehension*. The RAND Corporation.

Lane, H., & Contesse, V. (2022). *UFLI Foundations: An explicit and systematic phonics program*. Ventris Learning.

Lane, H., Pullen, P., Eisele, M., & Jordan, L. (2001). Preventing reading failure: Phonological awareness assessment and instruction. *Preventing School Failure, 46*, 101–110.

Lennox, S. (2013). Interactive read-alouds: An avenue for enhancing children's language for thinking and understanding: A review of recent research. *Early Childhood Education Journal, 41*(5), 381–389.

Liben, D. (2013, Winter). Which words do I teach and how? *The significance of vocabulary in the Common Core State Standards for ELA/Literacy*.

Liben, D., & Liben, M. (2019). *Know better, do better: Teaching the foundations so every child can read*. Learning Sciences International.

Liben, D., & Liben, M. (2024). *Know better, do better: Comprehension: Fueling the brain with knowledge, vocabulary, and rich language*. Scholastic.

Liben, D., & Paige, D. (2016). *What is reading fluency?* Achieve the Core.

Liben, M., & Pimentel, S. (2018). *A short guide to placing text at the center of learning*. Achieve the Core.

Liben, M., & Pimentel, S. (2018). *Placing text at the center of the standards-aligned ELA classroom*. Achieve the Core.

Lindsey, J. B. (2022). *Reading above the fray: Reliable, research-based routines for developing decoding skills*. Scholastic.

Lovejoy, E. (2023, January 26). *Brain bulletin #1: Simplifying the brain*. Express Readers.

Mann, V., & Singson, M. (2003). Linking morphological knowledge to English decoding ability: Large effects of little suffixes. *Neuropsychology and Cognition*.

Mastrothanasis, K., Kladaki, M., & Andreou, A. (2023). A systematic review and meta-analysis of the readers' theatre impact on the development of reading skills. *International Journal of Educational Research Open, 4*, 100–243.

McKeown, M. G., Beck, I. L., Omanson, R. C., & Perfetti, C. A. (1983). The effects of long-term vocabulary instruction on reading comprehension: A replication. *Journal of Reading Behavior, 15*(1), 3–18.

Medo, M. A., & Ryder, R. J. (1993). The effects of vocabulary instruction on readers' ability to make causal connections. *Reading Research and Instruction, 33*(2), 119–134.

Mesmer, H. A. (2019). *Letter lessons and first words: Phonics foundations that work*. Heinemann.

Miles, K. P., & Ehri, L. C. (2019). Orthographic mapping facilitates sight word memory and vocabulary learning. *Reading Development and Difficulties*, 63–82.

Moats, L. C. (1998). Teaching decoding. *American Educator*, Summer, 1–9. Available at http://www.aft.org/pdfs/americaneducator/springsummer1998/moats.pdf

Moats, L., & Tolman, C. (2019). *Language essentials for teachers of reading and spelling (LETRS)*. (3rd ed.). Voyager Sopris.

National Institute of Child Health and Human Development, NIH, DHHS. (2010). *Developing early literacy: Report of the National Early Literacy Panel*. U.S. Government Printing Office.

National Reading Panel. (2000). *Teaching children to read: An evidence-based assessment of the scientific research literature on reading and its implications for reading instruction*. National Institute of Child Health and Human Development.

Ness, M. (2024). *Read-alouds for all learners: A comprehensive plan for every student, every day*. Solution Tree Press.

Novelli, C., & Sayeski, K. L. (2022). Using sound walls to promote independent spellers. *TEACHING Exceptional Children*.

Orkin, M., Vanacore, K., Rhinehart, L., Gotlieb, R., & Wolf, M. (2022). The more you know: How teaching multiple aspects of word knowledge builds fluency skills. *The Reading League Journal, 2*(3), 4–13.

Pappas, C. (2014). *Instructional design models and theories: Schema theory*. eLearning Industry. https://elearningindustry.com/schema-theory

PaTTAN (Pennsylvania Training and Technical Assistance Network). (2019). *Effective practices for teaching academic vocabulary*.

Patton-Terry, N., & Connor, C. (2010). African American English and spelling: How do second graders spell dialect-sensitive features of words? *Learning Disability Quarterly, 33*, 199–210.

Pearson, P. D. (2009). The roots of reading comprehension instruction. In S. E. Israel and G. G. Duffy (Eds.), *Handbook of research on reading comprehension*. Routledge.

Peng, P., Wang, W., Filderman, M. J., Zhang, W., & Lin, L. (2023). The active ingredient in reading comprehension strategy intervention for struggling readers: A Bayesian network meta-analysis. *Review of Educational Research, 94*(2), 228–267.

Perfetti, C. A., Rieben, L., & Fayol, M. (Eds.). (1997). *Learning to spell: Research, theory, and practice across languages*. Lawrence Erlbaum.

Piasta, S. B. (2023). The science of early alphabet instruction. In S. Q. Cabell, S. B. Neuman, and N. Patton Terry (Eds.), *Handbook on the science of early literacy*. Guilford Press.

Piasta, S. B., & Hudson, A. K. (2022). Key knowledge to support phonological awareness and phonics instruction. *The Reading Teacher, 76*(2), 201–210.

Pimentel, S., Liben, D., & Liben, M. (2023). *Scaling the dinosaur effect: Topic vs. theme in elementary classrooms*. Knowledge Matters Campaign.

Pittman, R. T., Rice, M., Garza, E., & Guerra, M. J. (2023). The importance of phonemic awareness instruction for African American students. *The Reading League Journal*, 27–32.

Prescott, J. (2015). *The power of readers' theater: An easy way to make dramatic changes in kids' fluency, writing, listening, and social skills.* Scholastic. https://morethanenglish.edublogs.org/files/2015/03/The-Power-of-Readers-Theater-Scholastic.com-1afahe4.pdf

Price, L. H., van Kleeck, A., & Huberty, C. J. (2009). Talk during book sharing between parents and preschool children: A comparison between storybook and expository book conditions. *Reading Research Quarterly, 44*(2), 171–194.

Rasinski, T., (2004). *Creating fluent readers.* ASCD. https://www.ascd.org/el/articles/creating-fluent-readers

Rasinski, T., Ellery, V., & Oczkus, L. (2015). *Staying literacy strong: A focus on phrasing.* Literacy Now.

The Reading League. (2023). The Reading League curriculum evaluation guidelines. https://www.thereadingleague.org/curriculum-evaluation-guidelines

Reading Rockets. (n.d.). *Anticipation guides.* https://www.readingrockets.org/classroom/classroom-strategies/anticipation-guide

Reading Rockets. (n.d.). *List-group-label.* https://www.readingrockets.org/classroom/classroom-strategies/list-group-label#:~:text=List%2Dgroup%2Dlabel%20is%20a,relation%20to%20previously%20learned%20concepts

Recht, D. R., & Leslie, L. (1988). Effect of prior knowledge on good and poor readers' memory of text. *Journal of Educational Psychology, 80*(1), 16–20.

Reutzel, D. R. (2015). Early literacy research. *The Reading Teacher, 69*(1), 14–24.

Rice, M., Erbeli, F., Thompson, C. G., Sallese, M. R., & Fogarty, M. (2022). Phonemic awareness: A meta-analysis for planning effective instruction. *Reading Research Quarterly, 57*(4), 1259–1289.

Senechal, M., Ouellette, G., & Lam Nguyen, H. N. (2023). Invented spelling: An integrative review of descriptive, correlational, and causal evidence. In S. Q. Cabell, S. B. Neuman, and N. Patton Terry (Eds.), *Handbook on the science of early literacy.* Guilford Press.

Shanahan, T. (2005). *The National Reading Panel report: Practical advice for teachers.* Learning Point Associates.

Shanahan, T. (2014). *Should we teach students at their reading levels?* Reading Today.

Shanahan, T. (2016). *Does independent reading time during the school day create lifelong readers?* Shanahan on Literacy.

Shanahan, T. (2016). *Teaching comprehension and comprehension strategies.* Shanahan on Literacy.

Shanahan, T. (2018). *Comprehension skills or strategies: Is there a difference and does it matter?* Shanahan on Literacy.

Shanahan, T. (2018). *Should reading be taught whole class or small group?* Shanahan on Literacy.

Shanahan, T. (2018). *Should we teach with decodable text?* Shanahan on Literacy.

Shanahan, T. (2018). *What should morphology instruction look like?* Shanahan on Literacy.

Shanahan, T. (2019). *Does text structure instruction improve reading comprehension?* Shanahan on Literacy.

Shanahan, T. (2019). *Five things every teacher should know about vocabulary instruction.* Shanahan on Literacy.

Shanahan, T. (2019). *How decodable do decodable texts need to be? What we teach when we teach phonics.* Shanahan on Literacy.

Shanahan, T. (2019). Why children should be taught to read with more challenging texts. *Perspectives on Language and Literacy.*

Shanahan, T. (2021). *RIP to advanced phonemic awareness.* Shanahan on Literacy.

Shanahan, T. (2021). *Should we build a (word) wall or not?* Shanahan on Literacy.

Shanahan, T., & Lonigan, C. (2016). The role of early oral language in reading comprehension. *Improving Literacy and Communication Language Magazine.*

Smith, R., Snow, P., Serry, T., & Hammond, L. (2021). The role of background knowledge in reading comprehension: A critical review. *Reading Psychology, 42*(3), 214–240.

Stahl, S. A. (2005). Four problems with teaching word meanings (and what to do to make vocabulary an integral part of instruction). In E. H. Hiebert and M. L. Kamil (Eds.), *Teaching and learning vocabulary: Bringing research to practice.* Lawrence Erlbaum.

Stahl, S. A., & Fairbanks, M. M. (1986). The effects of vocabulary instruction: A model-based meta-analysis. *Review of Educational Research, 56*(1), 72–110.

Stahl, S. A., & Heubach, K. M. (2005). Fluency-oriented reading instruction. *Journal of Literacy Research, 37*(1), 25–60.

Stanovich, K. E. (1986). Matthew effects in reading: Some consequences of individual differences in the acquisition of literacy. *Reading Research Quarterly, 21*(4), 360–407.

Stollar, S. (2020). Six steps to start with sound walls. *Reading Science Academy.*

Sweller, J. (1988). Cognitive load during problem solving: Effects on learning. *Cognitive Science, 12*(2), 257–285.

Tatum, A. [@alfredtatum]. (2017, September 17). *Leveled texts lead to leveled lives.* AWT. View https://twitter.com/AlfredTatum/status/909563807525216256 [Post]. X.

Topping, K. J. (2014). Paired reading and related methods for improving fluency. *International Electronic Journal of Elementary Education, 7*(1), 57–70.

Vadasy, P. F., Sanders, E. A., & Cartwright, K. B. (2022). Cognitive flexibility in beginning decoding and encoding. *Journal of Education for Students Placed at Risk, 28*(4), 412–438.

van Rijthoven, R., Kleemans, T., Segers, E., & Verhoeven, L. (2021). Response to phonics through spelling intervention in children with dyslexia. *Reading & Writing Quarterly, 37*(1), 17–31.

Virginia Tech Center for Excellence in Teaching and Learning. (n.d.). *Activating prior knowledge.* Virginia Polytechnic Institute and State University.

Washington, J. A., & Seidenberg, M. S. (2021). Teaching reading to African American children. *American Educator.*

Washington, J. A., Lee-James, R., & Stanford, C. B. (2023). Teaching phonemic and phonological awareness to children who speak African American English. *The Reading Teacher 76*(6), 765–774.

Wexler, N. (2020). Building knowledge. *American Federation of Teachers.*

Wexler, N. (2022). *Elementary classrooms are too noisy for kids to learn.* Forbes.

Wexler, N. (2023). *No, teachers don't have to choose between knowledge and strategies.* Forbes.

Wiggins, A., Parker, J., White, B., & Schweld, J. (2020). Equitable ELA instruction: Immersing students in grade-level reading & thinking. *UnboundEd.*

Willingham, D. (2006). How knowledge helps. *American Federation of Teachers.*

Willingham, D. (2006). Knowledge in the classroom. *American Federation of Teachers.*

Willingham, D., & Lovette, G. (2014). Can reading comprehension be taught? *Teachers College Record.*

Wise, J. C., Sevcik, R. A., Morris, R. D., Lovett, M. W., Wolf, M., Kuhn, M., Meisinger, B., & Schwanenflugel, P. (2010). The relationship between different measures of oral reading fluency and reading comprehension in second-grade students who evidence different oral reading fluency difficulties. *Language, Speech, and Hearing Services in Schools, 41*(3), 340–348.

Wolf, M. (2007). *Proust and the squid: The story and science of the reading brain.* Harper Perennial.

Yopp, H. K. (1992). Developing phonemic awareness in young children. *The Reading Teacher, 45*(9), 696–703.

Young, C., Mohr, K. A. J., & Landreth, S. (2020). Improving boys' reading comprehension with readers theatre. *Journal of Research in Reading, 43*(3), 347–363.

Young, C., Paige, D., & Rasinski, T. V. (2022). *Artfully teaching the science of reading.* Routledge.

Zorfass, J., Gray, T., & PowerUp WHAT WORKS. (n.d.). *Connecting word meaning through semantic mapping.* Reading Rockets.

Zutell, J., & Rasinski, T. V. (1991). Training teachers to attend to their students' oral reading fluency. *Theory Into Practice, 30*, 211–217.

INDEX

Put the Science of Reading Into Practice

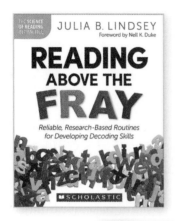

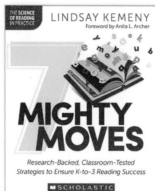

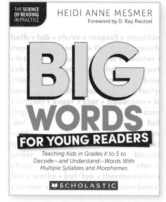

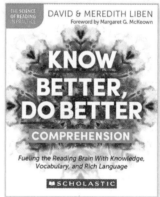

The science of reading is complex, but putting it into practice doesn't have to be. Our Science of Reading in Practice series empowers teachers by providing research-backed, classroom-tested strategies they can easily implement to transform literacy instruction.